aikido basics

Aikido

BASICS

Sensei Phong Thong Dang
Sixth-Degree Black Belt Aikikai
Founder of Tenshinkai Aikido

and

Lynn Seiser, Ph.D.
Third-Degree Black Belt Tenshinkai Aikido

TUTTLE PUBLISHING
Tokyo • Rutland, Vermont • Singapore

Published in the United States in 2003 by Tuttle Publishing, an imprint of Periplus Editions (HK) Ltd., with editorial offices at 364 Innovation Drive, North Clarendon, Vermont 05759 USA.

Library of Congress Catalog Card Number 2003054004

Dang, Phong Thong, 1940-
  Aikido Basics / Phong Thong Dang and Lynn Seiser. — 1st ed.
    p. cm.
  Includes bibliographical references.
  ISBN 0-8048-3490-3 (pbk.)
  1. Aikido. I. Seiser, Lynn, 1950- II. Title.

GV1114.35.P46 2003
796.815'4—dc21

ISBN 978-0-8048-3490-2

Distributed by:

North America, Latin America & Europe
Tuttle Publishing
364 Innovation Drive
North Clarendon, VT 05759-9436 U.S.A.
Tel: 1(802) 773-8930 Fax: 1(802) 773-6993
info@tuttlepublishing.com
www.tuttlepublishing.com

Asia Pacific
Berkeley Books Pte. Ltd.
61 Tai Seng Avenue #02-12
Singapore 534167
Tel: (65) 6280-1330   Fax: (65) 6280-6290
inquiries@periplus.com.sg
www.periplus.com

Japan
Tuttle Publishing
Yaekari Building, 3rd Floor
5-4-12 Osaki, Shinagawa-ku
Tokyo 141-0032
Tel: (81)3 5437-0171   Fax: (81)3 5437-0755
tuttle-sales@gol.com

First edition
13 12 11 10 09   10 9 8 7 6 5
Printed in Singapore

TUTTLE PUBLISHING® is a registered trademark of Tuttle Publishing, a division of Periplus Editions (HK) Ltd.

Dedication

I would like to dedicate this book to the founder of aikido, O'Sensei Morihei Ueshiba, his late son Doshu Kisshomaru Ueshiba, and his grandson, the current Doshu Moriteru Ueshiba. I also dedicate this book to everyone at the Aikikai Foundation and the Aikikai Hombu Dojo, especially General Secretary Shihan Masatake Fujita, for all their support and encouragement. I dedicate this book to my late brother, Tri Sensei, for sharing our dedication to the martial arts and for bringing aikido to my homeland, Vietnam. To all my students worldwide, I thank you for your enthusiasm in training. To my loving family, I thank you for your patience in my absences. It is my sincere wish that this book be some small contribution to unifying aikido.

—Phong Thong Dang, Westminster, CA
December 15, 2002

First, I dedicate this book, in humble gratitude and deepest respect, to the patience, compassion, and expertise of my aikido teacher, Sensei Phong Thong Dang. I also dedicate this work to all my training partners, past, present, and future, for their assistance and friendship. The lessons I have learned from them are humbly included in this book with my gratitude. My heartfelt love, deepest appreciation, and sincerest sympathies to my family for supporting my passion as a lifelong perpetual student of the martial arts.

—Lynn Seiser, Ph.D., Irvine, CA
December 15, 2002

The authors wish to express their appreciation to Joe Duong Dihn and Richmond Neff for their assistance by appearing in the photographs.

table of contents

part 1
introduction

AIKIDO is a unique martial art that combines the techniques of a variety of martial arts forms with a strong spiritual belief in love, peace, and harmony. As a result of this unique combination, aikido is beautiful and flowing, yet also a powerful and effective martial art.

Because aikido is made up of these two distinct elements—the technique and the spirit—people are often drawn to one aspect of the art more than the other at first. Some people are looking to aikido as a means of personal growth and spiritual transformation, while others are drawn to the flowing, powerful, and effective movements of aikido technique. What one discovers after dedicated practice is that these two seemingly separate elements are really interconnected, so that the spirit is discovered through practice of technique, and technique is improved when the spirit is embraced.

chapter 1
the history
of aikido

AIKIDO is a modern Japanese martial art that combines the traditional values of the warrior—through effective and efficient martial arts techniques—with the modern ethics of love and peace. Aikido is a nonviolent, noncompetitive martial art that offers a new model for conflict prevention, management, and resolution, as well as a means to practice personal and social responsibility.

Aikido was developed by Morihei Ueshiba in the early to mid-twentieth century. It is a relatively new martial art, but it has the appearance and code of honor of traditional martial arts.

Who Created Aikido?

Aikido was developed by Morihei Ueshiba (1883–1969), who is now affectionately called O'Sensei. His goal was to develop a martial art that would meet the needs of contemporary people. His prime concern was his love of traditional martial arts, his attempts to overcome misunderstandings about them, and his desire to reestablish their spiritual quality.

The development of aikido was Morihei Ueshiba's lifework, and he dedicated himself to the creation of aikido early in life. After watching young village hoods beat his father for his political views, he vowed to become strong enough to handle them someday. With that first vow, he began his journey into *budo*, the martial sciences. He studied and was influenced by many forms of martial arts, including Tenshin Shin'yo-ryu jujitsu, Shinkage-ryu swords, Yahyu-ryu jujitsu, judo, and especially Daito-ryu jujitsu.

Morihei Ueshiba's reputation grew as he studied. This reputation attracted

O'Sensei Morihei Ueshiba

numerous challengers, and after he defeated many of these opponents, some became his students. On one occasion, a young naval officer came to visit the small school Morihei Ueshiba had built close to his home. O'Sensei Morihei Ueshiba attempted to explain his theories of fighting and of *aiki*, the concept of flowing or harmonizing with the energy of an attack rather than resisting it. But the young officer had come to challenge and fight, not to listen. Finally, Morihei Ueshiba consented to the fight. Each time the officer attacked with his wooden sword, Morihei Ueshiba easily dodged the weapon by blending with it, or moving with the line of trajectory, rather than resisting it, and was easily able to evade repeated attacks without injuring his opponent.

After a lifetime of study, he was able to unbalance and throw opponents without body contact. He was able to quickly assess his attackers' vulnerable points and defeat them. This became the basis of aikido: the ability to use an opponent's movements and energy in order to protect yourself and others.

After considering many names, O'Sensei Morihei Ueshiba named his unique art aikido in 1941, after a lifetime of training in other martial arts. He studied over 200 martial arts styles in his lifetime. Aikido was his gift to humanity of blending the martial aspects of training the body with the spiritual aspects. He believed aikido to be the spirit of loving protection for all beings and the cure for a sick and violent world.

Who Carries on the Aikido Tradition?

The leadership of aikido was passed from father to son in 1969, when the third son of O'Sensei Morihei, Kisshomaru Ueshiba (1921–1999), was named aikido *doshu*

Kisshomaru Ueshiba, second doshu

Moriteru Ueshiba, third doshu

(leader or keeper of the way) and chairman of the Aikikai Foundation. Many attribute a more formalized training curriculum to Doshu Kisshomaru Ueshiba.

In 1999 the son of Doshu Kisshomaru Ueshiba and grandson to O'Sensei Morihei Ueshiba, Moriteru Ueshiba, became the aikido doshu after his father's death. Born in 1951, Doshu Moriteru Ueshiba graduated in 1976 from Meiji Gakuin University, became master of the Aikido World Head-quarters in 1986, and in 1996 became the chairperson of the Aikikai Foundation.

Aikido enjoys international growth and acceptance as a martial art and a means of personal transformation.

Today, we can say that aikido is different from other martial arts in that its goal is to defeat opponents by unbalancing them, rather than harming them. Aikido is also different in that its modernization has not led the art into being a competitive sport with contests and tournaments, or ranks based on win-ning.

chapter 2
the philosophy
of aikido

MANY OF THE TECHNIQUES of aikido originated in other martial arts that O'Sensei Morihei Ueshiba studied, but what makes aikido unique is its strong philosophical and spiritual base. Aikido is not just about how you move your body, it is also about moving your mind. The mind must learn to let go of a warlike philosophy of hate and fear, common to most martial arts, and embrace a loving philosophy of peace and harmony. The paradox of combining a martial art and a loving philosophy demonstrates that inclusion is much more powerful than exclusion: When the power of love and the power of martial arts are combined, the result is far more powerful than either could be alone.

At first, it would seem that an opponent and a defender are in two distinctly different positions, yet neither position could exist without the other. Understanding, accepting, and harmonizing this relationship to each other, instead of accepting the separation and difference from each other, is what makes aikido's philosophy unique.

Before O'Sensei Morihei Ueshiba's creation of aikido, the concept of attack and defense formed the basis of most martial arts. Aikido was the first Japanese martial art in which the actual training practice, application of technique, and philosophical foundation all work together.

Philosophical Principles of Aikido

Philosophically, aikido began as, and continues to be, a martial art. The goal of traditional Japanese martial arts is victory on the battlefield. History teaches us that such victories are very short-lived, however; they only lead to more fear, resentment, and eventual retaliation. The goal of aikido is victory over self, rather than victory over others.

Aikido is a martial art, a way of fighting. Aikido is budo, the way of war. Aikido is also the philosophical way of peace by promoting nonviolent conflict prevention, management, and resolution.

The symbol of traditional Japanese warfare is the sword, and many of aikido's unarmed techniques come directly from the art of sword fighting. Some traditional schools teach the sword movements before the unarmed movements, but this is to give students a sense of how the movement or technique should be done. The practice of sword techniques helps students to appreciate the origin of the technique within an armed fighting context, illustrates a practical application, and demonstrates the principles of aikido in action. The sword master's fluid skill shows the total coordination of a well-executed aikido technique. Every movement is carefully practiced and precise, using every part of the body and mind.

This unification of body and mind is one of the reasons that aikido is a spiritual discipline, as well as a martial art. By realizing that all of their movements must come together in the present action, students of aikido become aware that they can be one with everything around them.

Aikido teaches the philosophy that victory over one's self is more important than victory over others.

This emphasis on the philosophy, or worldview, of aikido often makes understanding the art difficult for the beginning student. On one level, the student of aikido must adopt a worldview that accepts violence and attacks. On the other hand, aikido does not meet like with like—aikido does not retaliate with more violence and attacks. It is easier to understand the details, or more subtle qualities, of aikido by first understanding the larger picture that they fit in. The basic techniques of aikido demonstrate the principles and philosophies of aikido; they illustrate, and make practical, aikido's underlying, ever-present philosophical concepts and generalizations.

Budo: The Way of War

The first philosophical term one should understand is *budo*. *Do* translates as "way" or "path." *Bu* translates as "martial." Budo is the "martial way" or "martial

arts." True budo has more to do with protection than victory. Warriors do not fight so
fiercely because they hate the enemy; they
fight fiercely because they love the people
they protect. Many modern martial arts
schools and media presentations miss this
underlying motivation, the positive intent
that was so important to O'Sensei Morihei
Ueshiba's vision and dream. Aikido is an extension of the budo code of love and respect
for others, and is also a means of self-disci-
pline. Training in aikido stresses cooperation,
not competition, between training partners.

> The word *ai* is a Japan-
> ese term which means
> "to harmonize," to enter
> and blend with an attack.
> The philosophy of ai
> encourages us to accept
> and live with an apprecia-
> tion of our differences.
> Aikido encourages the
> philosophy of accepting
> personal and social
> responsibility.

Ai: Harmony

Ai can be translated as meaning "harmony," "unity," or "to join and become
one." The concept of harmony in combat is hard for most people to compre-
hend. We are all used to fighting force with force, to meeting attack with resistance. The idea of meeting an attack with love and harmony appears
contradictory and impossible.

Within the concept of harmony is the necessity for difference. Music is the
easiest example to illustrate this. For harmony to occur, two or more different
notes must exist. There must be a certain interval between notes, usually a 1-
3-5-7 spacing. Together the notes produce one chord—in essence, the different
vibrations combine and become one chord. Discord happens when the notes
are not at a proper distance from each other. The concept of distance, referred
to as *ma-ai* in aikido, refers to the ability to combine with another's energy of
attack in a way that is the behavioral equivalent of musical harmony. While
you may not be in control of your attacker's position at first, you are in control of your distance, or interval, from him. As in music, when you change the
position, or distance, from the attacker to the defender, you can turn discord
into harmony.

Ki: Energy, Spirit, and Life

Ki translates as "spirit," "energy," "essence of life," "life force," and "universal
energy." Energy is also the power to act, lead, affect, or respond. The goal of
aikido is to harmonize the ki of the individual with the universal ki. The

The word *ki* is the Japanese term used to describe "energy" and "spirit." It is similar to the Chinese word *chi*, which refers to the energy that flows through the meridians as used in acupuncture and practiced in tai chi and chi kung. This philosophical concept exists in all forms of martial, philosophical, psychological, and spiritual practices. It is also considered the tangible force that exists in and guides all things.

energy within is the same as the energy without. An *aikidoka*, a practitioner of aikido, enters and blends with the universal ki through training. This allows him to feel the ki of an approaching opponent, to sense his energy before he comes into range, and to enter and blend to avoid harm. In this context, enter and blend mean to move along with the line of momentum of an attack. With practice, an experienced aikidoka can sense or detect the attack before physical contact is made. It is as if through training, the aikidoka reads the energy, or ki, of his attacker and can "roll along with it."

It is actually quite easy to illustrate this sensing of ki. We have all had the experience of sitting down next to somebody and feeling his or her bad mood. The more intense the feelings, the farther out the energy seems to travel, and the easier it is to actually sense it from across the room. Positive emotions have the same effect, but instead of pushing people away they draw us to them. We all like to be around someone who is positive. If both positive and negative ki is expressed and felt, then you have to choose which you send away and which you let in.

The essence of all life is breath, and ki is closely associated with the breath. Your breathing rate and depth change with both your emotional and physical experiences. Breath is one of the few automatic systems of the body that we can take conscious control over. Fluid, relaxed breathing is necessary for the proper execution of aikido techniques. The aikido practitioner inhales as a training partner approaches, creating a breath vacuum, or emptiness, to receive the partner's ki. The aikido practitioner exhales with the execution of movements and throws. This adds a dimension of ki into the *kokyu-nages*, or breath throws.

Ki, as energy, exists in all things and is the common element linking us all together. Ki allows us to feel connected with one another. Ki training develops your sensitivity to the movement of others and to your own power, by connecting and harmonizing the ki.

Do: The Way, or Path

It is often through a life of discipline that one finds the way of nature and the natural course that the essence of all things follows. This principle of *do* is the way into, and beyond, your individual life to what is natural and universal. Do is the basis of personal identity and the loss of that identity into the greater way of the universe. The awareness of the greater way is the basis of spirituality in aikido.

> The word *do*, similar to the Chinese word *tao*, represents an underlying universal way in which nature works. It is believed that to be aligned and congruent with this natural way will ensure power and victory.

The imagery most often used is that of water. Water does not need to decide what direction to flow. It simply follows the natural lines of geography. It uses the principle of gravity and flows to the lowest point, along the line of least resistance. Having the way of water allows you to have the flexibility to flow around obstacles without direct confrontation. Yet, if confrontation occurs, water has the ability to wear down even the toughest rocks to forge great valleys and canyons.

Omoto: The Great Origin, or Beginning

O'Sensei Morihei Ueshiba was spiritual by nature and a follower of the Omoto religion. *Omoto* literally translates to "great origin." It was a new religious sect founded by an illiterate, but enlightened, woman named Nao Deguchi (1871–1947). This Shinto sect picked up popularity during the early twentieth century until the Japanese government suppressed the movement, destroyed their property, and imprisoned their leader. O'Sensei Morihei Ueshiba became a believer in 1919 and maintained his relationship with them until his death in 1969. Many consider the influence of the Omoto religion to be the philosophical and spiritual foundation of aikido.

The philosophy of the Omoto religion forms the spiritual beliefs of aikido. These philosophies apply and govern life both inside and outside of the formal aikido training hall.

The four teachings and four principles, or rules, of the Omoto religion influenced O'Sensei Morihei Ueshiba and the development of aikido. The divine plan teaches human beings to lead a significant life. The basic teachings are (1) to harmoniously align ourselves with life and the universe, (2) to receive a revelation of celestial truth and its lessons, (3) to know the innate patterns of behavior for man, society, and the cosmos, and (4) to become aware of our instinctual creative drives. The four fundamental principles are (1) to gain purity of mind and body, (2) to maintain our optimism by believing in the goodness of the divine will, (3) to strive for progressive social improvement, and (4) to find the unification and reconciliation of all dichotomies. These principles are manifested throughout the universe. By practicing them, an individual can live in harmony with the universe and lead a heavenly life in spirit and body.

Some would say that the experience of war is what prompted O'Sensei Morihei Ueshiba to remove the deadly strikes from aikido. Others would say that it was the spiritual awakening of his Omoto faith that led him to devise an art of resolving conflicts aligned with philosophical and spiritual truths.

Sangen: The Triangle, Square, and Circle

 The triangle, square, and circle are central to the philosophy of aikido, and symbolize important aspects of the art. The triangle represents fire and water, and symbolizes various trinities such as mind-body-spirit and past-present-future. The triangle represents the flow of ki and a stable physical posture. The circle is the universal symbol for infinity, eternity, serenity, and perfection. The circle is fluid with no beginning and no end. As you accept and understand the principle of the circle, you will find that it is big enough to apply to your whole life, yet small enough to apply to your aikido techniques. The square is stability, order, and applied control. Together, they represent and symbolize the interrelatedness and harmony of humankind (triangle), earth (square), and heaven (circle).

Another interpretation (Dobson and Miller 1993, p. 153) uses the triangle, square, and circle to illustrate different ways to handle conflict. Attack is always fear-based because, without some type of fear, there would be no reason to attack. The triangle represents an attack. Two triangles, facing point-to-point, represent the fight response. A triangle facing away from another triangle (the original attack) represents the flight response. Flight is also fear-based. The freeze response, another fear-based response, is a square just

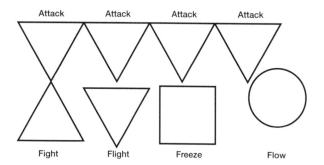

sitting there letting the triangle attack. It is only the circle that blends and flows with the attacking triangle. The circle blends with the attack by not directly resisting it but moves out of the way in a spiraling circular pattern along the triangle's line of attack. This is both symbolically and literally the way aikido faces conflict.

 O'Sensei's reason for combining effective martial arts techniques with a peaceful spiritual philosophy was to provide a way to transform our violent world.

The triangle represents the aikido ready stance, often referred to as the triangle stance because the feet are positioned as a triangle for balance. The triangle stance is established by placing the lead foot facing forward and the rear foot at a perpendicular ninety-degree angle slightly behind but aligned with the front foot's heel. This forms a triangle which provides balanced support and maneuverability. The circle represents the pivoting footwork (*tenkan*) that gives aikido its grace and power. The square represents points of balance and remaining firmly grounded. Enter with the sharp point of the triangle, move as a circle, and suppress with the firmness of the square (Fujita 1997, p. 24).

Beyond the Mat

The philosophical side of aikido, as a way of harmonizing spirit, is not only a way of war or fighting, but also a way of life. The consistent and persistent practice of aikido not only changes the way you move, but also the way you think.

Due to the nonaggressive philosophy underlying aikido, its benefits easily carry over into other areas of a practitioner's life outside the school. Aikido training teaches one to stay relaxed and calm in stressful situations, and to take things one step at a time. Already several books and organizations apply the

philosophy of aikido to other areas such as psychotherapy, education, relationships, mediation, and communication. After you have trained in basic
aikido for a time, you will begin to see the unique philosophy of aikido helping you in all areas of your life.

The learning and practice of aikido are ongoing. O'Sensei Morihei Ueshiba
was a great believer in continuous and repetitive practice. Eventually, as you
master the skills, you will discover the principles behind them. As you read
this book, you will find that some themes and points are consistently and con-
tinuously repeated. That is because learning takes continuous and repetitive
practice.

the different
branches of
aikido

THE NAME AIKIDO implies that there is only one art, the aikido of O'Sensei Morihei Ueshiba. However, those who studied with O'Sensei Morihei Ueshiba at different times learned different ways of illustrating the same aikido principles and techniques. Some of these students modified those ways and applications of techniques based on their own temperaments, physical limitations, and abilities. These differences have given rise to different styles of the same art of aikido.

There are two main styles stemming directly from the original aikido of O'Sensei Morihei Ueshiba: the original Aikikai emphasizes technique proficiency, and the newer Ki-Society emphasizes the development and extension of ki.

Different Branches

There are two major styles stemming from the original aikido of O'Sensei Morihei Ueshiba. The first is the Aikikai branch, directly affiliated with the Aikido World Headquarters, the Aikikai Foundation, and Aikikai Hombu Dojo, established by O'Sensei Morihei Ueshiba and his successors. The second, the Ki-Society style, is in affiliation and association with Sensei Kochi Tohei. Tohei Sensei was a top student and instructor under O'Sensei Morihei Ueshiba.

Classical aikido is referred to as Aikikai, the organization of Aiki. Several different organizations teach variations of the Aikikai style. The Aikikai style of aikido places great emphasis on technical proficiency of technique. Tomiki aikido, or Tomiki Ryu, is a style originated by Kenji Tomiki, who imitated the sport of judo competition in the hopes of acceptance into the educational institutions. Yoseikan Budo, established by Master Minoru Mochizuki in Japan, is a style strongly influenced by judo. *Iwama* style aikido, as taught by Morihiro Saito, emphasizes the relationship of unarmed techniques executed with *ken* (wooden sword) and *jo* (wooden staff) movements. Sensei Gozo Shioda established Yoshinkan aikido, emphasizing self-defense applications. *Tenshinkai*, meaning the association of heavenly hearts, is the name given to the fluid and powerful style of aikido from Vietnam founded by master Phong Thong Dang.

There are many branches or styles of aikido, but there is only one aikido.

Koichi Tohei, a *dan* under O'Sensei Morihei Ueshiba, founded the Ki-Society in 1971 to reflect a different emphasis and curriculum. The Ki-Society, known as Shin Shin Toitsu aikido, means aikido with body and mind coordination. Tohei Sensei brought aikido to the United States at the request of O'Sensei in 1953. The Ki-Society style of aikido emphasizes the development and use of ki to remain calm and relaxed in stressful situations in daily life. The Ki-Society combines ki development and breathing exercises with soft, flowing aikido techniques. Seidokan aikido, founded by Roderick Koayashi in 1981, draws from Tohei Sensei's Ki-aikido but emphasizes a balanced practice of principles and techniques

While the emphasis of these two major branches of aikido is different, their basis and origin are the same. There may be several other styles, or branches, of aikido—too many to keep track of. Many independent schools have opened and are actively training students. Their styles may not be covered here, but their exclusion is not meant in any way to be disrespectful.

part 2
getting started

AN OLD SAYING tells us that a journey of a thousand miles begins with a single step. Your journey into the beauty and power of aikido will be like that thousand-mile journey. It is filled with fascinating and unique scenery and traveling (or training) companions.

The beginning step sets the direction of the journey. Getting started in your aikido training can be very difficult. As a beginner, you do not know what to look for and what questions to ask.

First of all, getting started in aikido means choosing a school, buying your first uniform, showing up for your first class, and training safely.

choosing the
right school

C HOOSING THE RIGHT aikido school for you is essential for both your practice and your personal development. There are many considerations to keep in mind. Here are some guidelines to help you on your search.

Finding Available Schools

To find the aikido school closest to you, check your local Yellow Pages. Many sites on the Internet offer school-search functions. These listings may be somewhat limited, however, so check martial arts supply stores in your area for business cards and flyers of local teachers and their schools. Check the local parks and recreation departments, the YMCAs, local health clubs, and community or state colleges, for possible classes or aikido clubs.

Your Goals and the School's

The first step is to realize who you, as a new student, are. An important aspect to consider is the ethics of your motivation for studying aikido, and the ethics of the school's motivation for teaching it. Why do you want to learn aikido? Are there specific aspects of the art that you are more interested in, and that you'd like your training to focus on? If your primary motivation is self-defense, for example, then your criteria for judging a school depend on that. Many aikido schools do not emphasize the self-defense aspects of training, but rather the development and transformation of the person. The focus of each aikido school may vary according to the style and the instructor. Some schools will focus on the development of ki over technical proficiency. Others will focus on more practical self-defense or weapons training. Just as you need to determine the focus of aikido that interests you, you'll also need to determine the focus of potential schools.

The right school is the one that best matches your reasons, motivation, and ethics. Therefore, it is important for new students to be clear about why they want to train in aikido and what they want to get out of that training. By asking these questions of yourself up front, you'll be better able to recognize the school that best suits your needs.

School Location

According to an old joke, success in business depends on three things: location, location, and location. Convenient location is an important consideration. If it is not easy to get to the school, you may not be able to get to class on a regular basis, which will hinder your training.

Class Schedule

Convenient class schedule is another important consideration. While some aikido schools offer classes at various times, others can be very limited in class meeting times and frequency. Many schools only offer classes during the evening, or only in the morning and on weekends. Try to find a school that provides classes that match your schedule.

Financial Responsibility

Training in aikido also comes with a financial commitment and responsibility. It is important to know up front what financial agreement and contract you will face as a new student. Many schools have a monthly rate with unlimited class attendance. Others have a monthly rate that only allows a certain amount of class time. Local service organizations and colleges charge fees on a course or semester basis. Some schools offer a special rate if you pay in advance for a "black belt" program—but many people drop out of training before reaching the black belt level. Ask yourself how much training is worth to you. How much can you afford? There are enrollment fees, dues, testing fees, clothing and equipment costs, and gas or other transportation expenses.

The Teacher

A major consideration for successful training is the competence of the instructor. Competence is more than just high rank and recognized affiliation. Competence means whether or not the instructor can teach. Can the head instructor actually convey the basics of aikido in a manner that makes them understandable and learnable? Does the head instructor actually teach the classes? It is common practice for a martial arts school to be established on the basis of the head instructor's rank and reputation, but the head instructor may actually teach very little. The beginning student can learn a great deal from assistant instructors, because they are advanced in their training, but the advanced student will want to train more directly with the head instructor. This is considered a great honor.

Class Size

Class size can be an important factor in finding the right school. Some students require instruction that is more personal, and prefer a smaller class size, while others like the social aspects of being involved in a larger group activity. The right class size will be the one that provides the best learning environment for you. No matter how large or small the class, however, there should be a sense of control and discipline at all times.

Atmosphere

The general atmosphere of the school and its classes should also be a consideration. Atmosphere takes into account how the students interact with each other. Aikido should be practiced cooperatively, not competitively. As a beginning student, you will be caught up in the atmosphere of the school. As you eventually become a senior student, it will be your responsibility, obligation, and privilege to help establish and maintain a positive atmosphere that is conducive to teaching and learning aikido.

Clutter and Cleanliness

The clutter or cleanliness of an aikido school indicates the teacher's desire to make a comfortable training place for students. Cleanliness has many health benefits, too. A school that is too cluttered, or not clean, indicates a cluttered and unkempt mind. The beginning student will feel more welcome in a clean, uncluttered school. The advanced student will take active responsibility for, and participate in, its cleanliness and upkeep.

Safety

Another important consideration is safety. Accidents and injuries do happen, but these are exceptions to the rule. There should always be a first aid kit available, and the instructors should have training in emergency first aid. Most injuries in aikido training can be avoided by taking training seriously, following instructions, using common sense, and relaxing.

Reliability

How long have the school and teacher been in the area? Perhaps more importantly, how long do they intend to stay in the area? Many schools open, attract new students, and then fail for one or more reasons. This leaves the new students with nowhere to train, after possibly paying many dues and fees up front.

Ethical Responsibility

First, last, and always, the ethical responsibility of the school and teacher is extremely important. Ethics are a set of guidelines established by a specific profession to govern the activities of people doing business within that field of expertise. This is separate from the legalities of a business practice. Very few martial arts instructors have taken business courses that teach them to run their business in ethical, yet profitable, ways. Many have been trained in the instructor/student relationship of traditional martial arts, which implies a lifelong commitment and responsibility to each other. In the Western world, where martial arts are more of a hobby taken up for health and entertainment reasons, the students only feel responsible for paying their fees and showing up for class. Likewise, instructors may feel that they are simply responsible for collecting fees and sharing some of their knowledge. Aikido teachers must be willing to accept that their ethical responsibility to the student extends far beyond the class or the school.

You will not only get the technical lessons from your instructor and the people you train with, you also learn their ethics and philosophy. Choose your training facility intelligently and wisely.

Once you find a school that is convenient in location and is affordable, you will need to assess if the techniques taught appear effective and learnable. Are the students having a good time while they train? In addition, how does the school treat its new students? As a new student, are you welcomed into the aikido community?

Before making any decision, it is important to visit several schools and watch their classes. It cannot be emphasized enough that you should gather as much information as possible about the school and the instructor. Whatever choice you make, don't stay with a school if you later find that the choice was not the right one for you. In traditional martial arts training, the choice of the right school and teacher is very important. This right choice can make the difference between frustration, humiliation, and quitting or finding a lifelong hobby, or way of life. The study of aikido has applications far beyond the school walls.

chapter 5

clothing and

equipment

AIKIDO REQUIRES appropriate clothing and equipment that will help you fit in and train properly.

Clothing

There are three basic personal requirements aside from the traditional uniform, or *dogi*: the belt, selected undergarments, and ultimately, the *hakama*.

Uniform (Dogi, or Gi)

The most important piece of equipment is the purchase of the dogi. The dogi, referred to as a *gi*, is the traditional martial arts uniform. It consists of a jacket and pants. The jacket is a wraparound, long-sleeved jacket without buttons, made of bleached cotton. The pants are often of the same material, with either a drawstring or elastic waist. Most pants have reinforced seams and a gusset

For many people, working out in a martial arts uniform is exciting. It is a statement that you have started your journey.

crotch for increased flexibility. The legs should not be so long that they drag on the ground. There are many styles and weight of dogi. Many students start with the less expensive, lightweight karate-style dogi. Advanced students prefer to wear the heavier judo-style dogi. Some dogi come with elaborate embroidering or calligraphy. Some schools sell their preferred dogi, while others include it in the enrollment cost.

The Belt

The belt wraps twice around the dogi and ties in front with a square knot. There are two ways to tie the belt. You can either start with a small section of the belt in front and then wrap the belt around you twice, over itself, before tying it in front. Another way is to start by holding the belt in front of you, with the middle at your center, and then wrap it around you until both ends are in front.

The belt represents more than something that holds your pants up and your top together. Your belt represents your rank and your training. People may ask what color belt you wear. Your dogi will last you for years, but with disciplined practice, you will earn a different belt of another color. In reality, however, the color of the belt is not as important as the skill and integrity of the person wearing it.

In the old schools, everyone wore a white belt until it became black. The old story is that if you do not wash your belt, it will go through a color change similar to the color rank system. Eventually, the belt will turn black. If you continue to train, the black belt becomes frayed, worn, faded, and will return to its original white state.

Don't take the color of your belt too seriously; it will change.

Undergarments

Many people find it useful and courteous to wear an undershirt under their gi while training. For many women, this becomes a means of maintaining a sense of modesty. Others appreciate the absorption quality of an undershirt. It is a personal preference.

Since aikido does not use strikes or kicks directly to the groin area, it is not necessary to wear any sort of groin protector. Wearing undergarments that provide some sense of support is useful and provides both safety and comfort.

The Hakama

The hakama is the formal pleated skirtlike pants worn by advanced students. The hakama symbolizes the accomplishment of many hours and years of training, dedication, and discipline. It is a status symbol in some schools. Some schools allow women to wear the hakama out of modesty. This comes from traditional Japanese culture, and should not be considered politically incorrect or sexist. Some modern schools do not make this exception, however.

There is a ritual for folding your hakama when you are finished training. It provides a time to reflect on your training and your purpose for taking aikido.

You may have some difficulties getting dressed at first. With time, putting your uniform on will be a part of your ritual for preparing your body and your mind for training. Your uniform will become a statement of who you are and what you will become. Wear it proudly.

Equipment

Your school will provide most of the equipment needed to practice aikido. The most important is the mat on which you will train. The mat provides a safe place to fall and roll while practicing the basic techniques.

The only pieces of equipment that you will eventually have to buy are your weapons. Weapons training begins at various times for the beginner in aikido. There are three primary weapons used in aikido training: the jo, or wooden staff; the *bokken*, or wooden sword; and the *tanto*, or wooden knife.

chapter 6
your first class

YOU HAVE ALREADY WATCHED a few classes, so you have some idea what you can expect. You have interviewed and chosen a school and teacher that you believe can provide you with the best training available. You have signed up, shown up, and suited up. You walk into the school for your very first class. Welcome to aikido, the way of peace and harmony.

Before Class

Expectations

A word of advice is not to have too many expectations. The plan you have in your mind may not be the plan your new teacher has for your first lesson. If you are not filled with your own expectations, you will be more open to whatever is offered. As a beginner, you will encounter several new things when you attend your first class. Some will be physical and some will be psychological.

Aikido is an art of humility. By looking at what you know, you will also discover how much you have to learn.

You may, at first, feel disappointed from a martial arts perspective, since aikido can look soft. As you study, however, you will find that the soft appearance gives way to the power of the throws and locks of aikido. With training, the softness returns but brings with it the power of the martial art. Aikido takes patience and persistent training. Eventually, your disappointments will turn to enjoyment and even amazement.

Humility

On first appearance, the techniques of aikido look simple to perform. When one actually tries to do them, however, they often turn out to be much more complicated than they seemed initially. The excitement you initially feel may give way to frustration when training actually begins. Be patient. With consistent and persistent training, the frustration is replaced by the even deeper excitement and appreciation for what aikido is, and for the skills you have gained.

Considering all that aikido encompasses, you should expect the first class to be overwhelming. Aikido keeps evolving and changing. Expect to change with it. Aikido has an infinite number of combinations of techniques that change with every encounter. Don't try to memorize everything too soon. Be patient with yourself and train hard. Eventually, the things that once overwhelmed you will become automatic.

Be Prepared and Show Up Early

It is considered disrespectful to show up after a class has begun. Arrive early to show that you respect the teacher, the school, your fellow students, and yourself. Have your uniform ready to go. Give yourself enough traveling time. Walk in, look around, and welcome yourself to your new home.

Introductions

Introduce yourself to others. Aikido practitioners are usually friendly. It is a way of practicing harmony and extending ki beyond the traditional practice on the mat. These strangers will become your friends, and most importantly, your training partners.

Almost everything in aikido starts and ends with a bow as a show of respect and humility.

The Start of Class

Bowing

Expect to bow in class a lot. Bowing, called *rei* in Japanese, is a form of greeting and respect. Bow when you first enter the school and when you first step on the mat.

At the beginning of the class, kneel and bow to a picture of O'Sensei Morihei Ueshiba. Bowing is not a religious gesture or ceremony that goes against anyone's faith of choice. Bowing to O'Sensei Morihei Ueshiba is simply thanking him and showing respect for what he has given to the aikido community. In the front of the training area, usually opposite to the entrance, is the *shomen*. This is traditionally a raised, or recessed, shrinelike structure that is a place for ancestral spirits to reside and watch over us as we practice. The shomen usually contains a picture, a scroll, and some plant or greenery to remind us of nature. The shomen is a way to remember and honor O'Sensei Morihei Ueshiba, as our ancestor, for giving us aikido as a physical and spiritual practice. The shomen becomes a focus of training.

Bow to your teacher. Learning respect, humility, gratitude, and appreciation is just one of the benefits you will gain through your study of aikido.

You will see people doing a simple standing bow. They may just put their hands at their sides and bend slightly at the waist. Others will put their hands in front and bow deeply. Some schools or teachers advocate keeping your eyes open and focused on your training partner as you bow. Watch how others are bowing, and follow their examples.

> *Getting used to the kneeling positions of aikido takes practice and patience. Your knees will appreciate your gentleness.*

Line Up, Kneel, and Bow

Line up according to rank. At your first class, you will more than likely be the one with the lowest rank. Take your place at the far left of the line, by sitting on your heels with your back straight. This is the traditional kneeling position. Relax and breathe. You will line up at the beginning and end of class, and quite possibly several times in between.

To assume the traditional kneeling and bowing positions, simply step forward and then lower yourself onto one knee. Bring your other knee onto the mat and align both knees. Sit on your heels. The toes can be curled under so the bottom of the toes and balls of the feet are on the mat. This position actually makes it easier to stand and respond if attacked. For formality, most people let the tops of their feet touch the mat. Some schools allow their students to sit with their knees apart. Others feel that this position is impolite and the knees should be together. Both hands rest, palms down, on the legs. The spine is straight. To bow, move the left hand forward onto the mat, follow it with the right hand, forming a triangle between the hands, and rock forward, letting the head dip down. Rock back up to a kneeling position. Return the right hand first, followed by the left hand, to their original position on the knees.

Listen

Expect to listen. Listen with your ears, your eyes, and most importantly, with your body. Hear what the teacher tells you and follow instructions. Listen with your eyes as the teacher demonstrates the techniques. Listen with your body by making subtle movements that mimic the movement being demonstrated.

Minimal Social Conversation

Stay focused on why you have decided to become involved in aikido. The social contacts and friends you make will be important to you for the rest of your life. There is time outside the school to cultivate these relationships. While in class, keep your social conversation to a minimum. Some schools prohibit social conversation during practice. You are here to train, not socialize. Minimize your talk and maximize your training. You will find it worthwhile.

Follow Instructions

Follow instructions to the best of your ability. What you are told to do will sound easy. What is demonstrated to you will look easy. Following instructions will make it easier for you, but remember, as a beginner in your first class, you are not expected to get it right. You are just expected to do your best. There are many subtleties in aikido. Many times, you will think you are doing exactly what you have seen the teacher demonstrate, and yet it doesn't seem to work. Following instructions will allow you to adjust your technique ever so slightly and discover that it works.

Behavior

Ask Questions

Most questions are answered through training. As a beginner, you will either be full of questions far beyond what you need to know for the level of your training, or you will not have the slightest clue about what to ask. An empty mind is the open mind of the beginner, and will be ready to receive learning. Accept the answer you receive. We often ask questions but do not really listen to the answers. Once you have an answer, return to your practice. Many times the words will make better sense if they are practiced though aikido movements.

Take Turns

Aikido is cooperative, interactive learning. You will learn to both give and receive the basic techniques of aikido. Your training partners will help you by allowing you to practice with them. You will reciprocate and allow them to practice with you. This partnership becomes a profound learning experience that extends far beyond the relationship you have in the school. After you have practiced a technique a few times with each hand, bow to your training partner and let him or her have a turn. Do not monopolize the training opportunity and time.

Always be polite. Aikido begins and ends with bowing to each other. Good manners are the first level of self-defense.

After Class

Gratitude and Appreciation

Expect to cultivate an attitude of gratitude and appreciation. You will appreciate the efforts made by others to show up and train with the discipline that has allowed them to advance and share their learning with you. You can look forward to the day when new students will appreciate, and be grateful for, what you will share with them.

Not Knowing

Aikido does not lend itself to easy description or definition, even by the best of practitioners. You may not totally remember what you learned. Learning will be gradual. There will always be more questions than answers in aikido. The beauty of the art is that it keeps refining and teaching you.

Exhaustion

Breath control is another factor of aikido that many beginning students do not anticipate. The cardiovascular aspects of being out of shape for the vigorous workout may leave you out of breath as well. As a new student, you will be taught to breathe normally while executing the aikido techniques and when taking the falls. Your cardiovascular fitness will increase over time. What once made you out of breath will later only take your breath away as you experience the beauty of aikido.

Soreness

Many new students find they are sore after their first class. You have used your body and muscles in ways you are not used to. The body takes a while to adjust and accommodate itself to the new workload. If you are in pain, it may mean that something has been injured. Talk to your teacher and consult with a medical care professional. Some soreness just means that you had a good workout and that you are taking your body beyond its normal limits. It means you are learning. You will learn eventually to relax and gain harmony with your body.

Now that you know what to anticipate in your first class, don't expect it to be exactly as described here. Each training partner you have will approach you with slightly different energy. You must be able to respond to each. This adaptability is essential to aikido. It is explicit in the teachings and implicit in the training.

chapter 7
safety

DESPITE ITS STRONG philosophical base and its emphasis on peace and harmony, aikido is a martial art. On first observing it, some will say they can see the gentleness in the art. Others witness the painful joint locks and hard landing on the mats. To them, aikido looks very violent. The practice of aikido requires a measure of safety, and there are safety rules and requirements for the environment in which you train.

Before any rigorous exercise program, consult your primary care physician. Physical illnesses and limitations known ahead of time can prevent injuries or reinjuries.

Aikido is based on the loving protection of all things. This includes yourself and your training partners. Everything you do in aikido should show a deep respect for potential harm. Always train with safety in mind.

Some Personal Safety Rules

There are many basic rules to follow that will make the training in aikido safer. Many of them are common sense.

No Horseplay

A basic safety rule is no horseplay. You may want to mimic some character from your favorite action movie. Your own bit of acting may get you some laughs from others, but ultimately, it will distract you and others from what you came to the school for—to learn aikido. Because aikido is a martial art, the techniques you will be practicing have the potential of inflicting great damage and harm. They must be practiced without horseplay·to minimize the likelihood that someone, possibly you, will get hurt. Enjoy your training, but remember it is not play.

Pay Attention

Pay attention to what your teacher tells you to do, and do it. Pay attention to your movements. Pay attention to your training partner's movements. Pay attention to the space around you. It is easy to get caught up in the momentum of your own training and forget that others are training next to you, and that they are more than likely caught up in their own training. This can create accidents as you both throw your training partners into the same space. The impact can be dangerous. Try to pay attention to where you throw your training partners and where they are falling. These awareness skills pay great dividends in the school as you practice aikido. These skills alone can be your first line of self-defense.

Other Safety Considerations

> Relaxing is one of the most important things you can do to prevent injuries and increase the effectiveness of you technique.

Relax

It is important to stay relaxed during your training. The usual response to stress is to tense up and stop breathing. Learning a new skill, especially one that incorporates joint locks and throws, could be considered stressful. Staying relaxed helps the body move freely and more fluidly. This relaxation actually prevents injuries.

Rolling and Falling (*Ukemi*)

It is impossible to practice aikido without learning how to take falls. This can be very frustrating. You may want to learn all the fancy throws and footwork that make aikido such a beautiful art, but learning how to fall is for your safety and the safety of your training partners. Falling is not just important in aikido, it is an essential necessity. Taking *ukemi* and learning to be a good training partner is as hard, if not harder, than learning the techniques of aikido.

First Aid

Injuries do happen. They cannot all be prevented. If injured, report it, clean it up, and clean yourself up. Your instructor needs to know if you are injured and can help to determine whether or not you need additional first aid or medical attention. How you react to injuries can affect healing and recovery. Many beginning students want to "tough it out" and train although they are injured. This is not wise training. The sooner an injury receives the proper diagnosis, the sooner you can begin proper treatment, which will help you make a faster recovery. If you accidentally injure your training partner, check on him or her and apologize. If a training partner accidentally injures you, offer your forgiveness and the reassurance that you are okay. Like you, your training partners are learning aikido. Train in peace and harmony.

Don't Train When You Are Ill, Injured, or Fatigued

It is not a safe practice to train if you are ill, injured, or too fatigued. If you are ill, you will not be able to pay attention to your instruction or training, and you may infect others at the school. This is considered disrespectful. If you train injured, you may complicate your injury and have to postpone training or stop altogether. If you are too fatigued, you will not pay attention and will get sloppy in your practice. Sloppiness causes accidents and injuries.

Warm Up

Always warm up before you train. Warming and stretching the muscles read-ies the body for a good workout. It is one of the best ways to train more safely and effectively.

Common Sense Is Wisdom

Remember that you are training in a martial art that ultimately can cause great harm. Always use your common sense. Train wisely and train safely.

Safety Requirements for the School

Mats

One of the most important pieces of safety equipment for any aikido school is a good mat. Good mats absorb the impact of a throw and absorb the mistakes

> You have a responsibility to yourself, your training part-ner, and your school to train safely. They have a responsibil-ity to make sure you do.

you or your training partners make. Mats should be in good condition. Since you practice barefoot, it is possible to get your toe caught or broken in a tear of a mat. Mats used today are softer and absorb more impact than the traditional tatami mats used in years past .

Ventilation

Good ventilation is a good safety precaution. The air you breathe is the fuel that runs your body. Stale air can breed bacteria and spread infection. Good ventilation helps keep the air fresh.

Lighting

At advanced stages, it may be stimulating to train in a darkened school—limiting the sense of sight helps you develop auditory (sound) and kinesthetic (feeling) awareness. However, in the beginning stages of learning aikido, it is very important to see what is being demonstrated for you, what you are doing, and what is being done to you. Good lighting makes for safer training.

Heating and Cooling

Common sense will tell you that it is not wise to train in a place that is too hot or too cold. The facility should have an adequate heating and cooling system. Fans are very useful and appreciated during the hot summer months.

Cleanliness

Cleanliness is a means of safety. Cleanliness prevents diseases and injuries, and provides a positive atmosphere and environment for training. As a beginning student, you may not feel responsible for the cleanliness of the school; you may only participate in the required sweeping of the mat before or after class. Eventually, however, as you progress, you too will take great pride in helping to provide a clean environment in which to train.

Just as the mat area should be clear and clean, so should the surrounding areas. There should be no beams, pillars, or radiators that are exposed and potentially dangerous. Anything on the walls should be well secured.

Restrooms and Changing Rooms

It is important to have bathroom facilities available. They should be clean and fully supplied with a toilet, a sink, hot and cold water, soap, and paper towels. Always wash your hands after leaving the restrooms.

Having changing rooms available also adds to the safety of the student. Most schools have separate changing rooms for males and females.

Water

Because your workout can be exhausting, the ability to rehydrate your body is an important safety feature. Most schools have a water cooler available. Many students bring their own drinks. Please remember to dispose of your paper cups or bottles appropriately.

Keep Equipment in Good Condition

To prevent injuries, all training equipment provided by the school, or by yourself, should be kept in good condition and repair.

Awareness and Vigilance

Awareness and vigilance are among the most important factors in safe training. A competent instructor will always be aware of and vigilant about what is going on. If you forget the basic rule of safety, a good instructor will remind you. Vigilant instructors who see some aspect of the training environment that needs attention or repair will see to it. They watch over you so you can train.

Safety is not just an issue for someone else. Your safety in training in aikido is the responsibility of yourself, your training partners, and your teacher. Take your role seriously. You can prevent injuries to yourself and others by using common sense, paying attention, and following the simple rules presented here.

part 3
learning the basics

WHERE DOES ONE START when learning aikido? When you stand and watch an aikido demonstration, it appears graceful and easy, yet its effects are magical and powerful. All artists start by learning the craft. The craft consists of the basic elements that make up the abilities and skills of your aikido repertory.

In the beginning, the techniques of aikido illustrate its underlying principles. In the end, the principles drive the techniques. Every movement will be a natural illustration and application of a natural principle. The techniques appear to work all by themselves.

The basics of aikido begin with knowing how to stand and move. All aikido techniques are based on full-body movement and unique footwork. As you progress in your aikido training you will be confronted with various attacks in the form of strikes and grabs. You will learn how to enter and blend with those attacks, using your footwork, and to redirect them into either throwing techniques or locking and pinning techniques.

chapter 8
basic principles

THE PRINCIPLES OF AIKIDO apply to your relationship with yourself and your relationship to your training partner. All aikido techniques are behavioral illustrations of these principles. The techniques become ways of seeing the principles in action. Once you have worked on the techniques, you will no longer think of them in terms of movement, but in terms of principles. In the end, you won't even think in terms of the principles, because they will become a part of you.

The relationship between you and your training partner best illustrates these principles. If you are the one practicing the technique, you are called *tori*. Your training partner, who receives the technique so you can practice, is referred to as *uke* or *nage*. As you practice, you will alternate between tori and uke. Such is the balance of aikido.

Important TrainingPrinciples

O'Sensei Morihei Ueshiba believed that those who want enlightenment never stop forging themselves. Words or theories cannot express the realizations of enlightenment. Perfect actions echo the patterns found in nature. The two most important principles to remember when practicing are to (1) enter and blend and (2) to break your training partner's balance point.

The General Sequence of Techniques

There is a general progressive process, or sequence, to aikido techniques. The first technique is to enter and blend with your training partner's approach or attack. The next is to redirect and unbalance the attacker. You then either use a throw or control your training partner with a pinning joint lock. Last, you let go and move on. Many say that the blending and taking of balance are the basis for all aikido techniques. Pay close attention to these two principles at all times.

In aikido, most of your training practice will be from a stationary position. You will stand there as your training partner approaches and attacks. You will walk through your technique in a sequential step-by-step fashion. This is where you start. Eventually, your training practice will become more dynamic and fluid. As your training partner approaches, in an attempt to attack, you will begin to enter and blend by moving with his momentum and inertia. The step-by-step process will become one step. Finally, the blending becomes a means to take your training partner's balance, and he or she will fall in response to your movement.

Two of the most important principles of aikido are blending (joining with an attack), and breaking balance (unbalancing your opponent).

Enter and Blend

"Enter and blend" means to flow with your training partner's approach or attack, rather than resist it. To enter means to move into the attack. Blending means to join it, become one with it. You will seldom be instructed to back up. You will be asked to step off the line of attack. You will be asked to move forward toward your training partner, or at least into the space next to him or her. This emptying of space allows your training partner to be carried by momentum to a point beyond the anticipated target without meeting resistance.

In judo and jujitsu—the latter being an art from which aikido derived many techniques—there is a saying that goes, "When pushed, pull, and when pulled, push." These movements were often linear in nature, pulling the opponent directly into you, or pushing yourself directly into the opponent. O'Sensei Morihei Ueshiba added the element of a circular step (tenkan), so that rather than following a direct linear course, the throw follows a downward spiraling motion that adds power to the throw and the impact.

Breaking Balance

There are several ways to determine the balance point of your training partner. If you were to drop an imaginary line directly down your centerline onto the ground, it would land at a point directly between your feet. At ninety degrees directly forward and back from that point, at about a shin's length, is the balance point. If you aim a technique toward this point, it will be easy to break your training partner's balance. Another way to determine your training partner's balance point is to measure, at a radius of a shin's length, a circle around each foot. If you extend that radius by allowing, or pulling, your training partner's range of motion to go past their full extension, he will lose his balance.

Emptying can be used to unbalance. To empty a space is to not physically be where your training partner expects you to be. As your training partner reaches for you, allow his hands to continue forward beyond the point where they anticipate impact. By not being there, you will cause your training partner to lose his mental focus and physically overextend beyond his balance point, losing his balance. When your training partner is off balance, he is very easy to move, control, and throw.

Relax

Stay relaxed as you practice. A relaxed body is often the sign of a more relaxed mind and an openness to learning. Resistance produces tension in the body. This tension creates rigidity in the muscles, which makes injuries more likely. You are less likely to get hurt if you are relaxed than if you are tense. At first, it will take some effort to stay relaxed during training. Eventually, however, you will experience and know both the power and the safety in maintaining a completely relaxed body.

Breathe

Inhale as you begin entering and blending. Exhale as you execute the technique. Always exhale as you take the fall, as uke. Remember to breathe during training, and exhale during ukemi. Learning a new skill can be stressful, and people under stress tend to hold their breath and need to be constantly reminded to breathe. Also, slow, deep, rhythmic breathing is a great way to stay calm and control your emotional state.

Enjoy Yourself

O'Sensei Morihei Ueshiba taught that aikido should be practiced with a joyous nature. That does not mean that one should fool around and not take practice seriously. It simply means to keep a positive attitude about the training and enjoy it. A positive attitude helps you to stay mentally focused, emotionally calm, and physically strong. Besides, nothing unbalances attackers more than to see a slight smile on your face when they are coming at you. Learning to maintain a positive attitude during training, when someone is attacking you, will help you cope with the everyday stressful situations at home, school, and work.

> *P*ractice physical alignment: when the right hand goes forward or back, so does the right foot. When the left hand goes forward or back, so does the left foot. Coordination of hands and feet will give full body power to your technique.

Maintain Physical Alignment

One of the easiest general rules about the physical alignment necessary for throws is to keep everything pointed in the same direction. Your feet, knees, hips, shoulders, and eyes should all point at, and through, your training partner's centerline. If you aim your alignment toward the opponent's balance point, you will add power to your technique.

Keep your hands in front of you, on your centerline. To keep your technique strong and avoid injury, keep your hands where you can see them. Don't let your arms get beyond the sides of your body. Keep your elbows pointed down and tucked in front of your body. Keep your arms and ki at a natural extension, as if pushing forward. Visualize the weight of your arms, on the underside of the arm. This lowers the arms' center of gravity and provides you with a sense of upward support. At the same time, think of your arms as unbendable by holding them with a springlike tension, with a slight curve at the elbow. Do not totally lock the elbow, since this produces rigidity rather than fluidity. Never collapse your arm beyond ninety degrees. This will weaken your technique.

Try to keep your hands at hip width apart. A good training visualization is to see your hands and your hips as the four corners of a square, which move together. As the hip goes forward or back, the hand on the same side goes forward or back. Keeping your hands and hips aligned helps coordinate the full-body movement characteristic of aikido.

Always stand straight. You should feel as if you are being lifted up, allowing your spine to elongate. Keep the body erect and straight. Hold a proud upright posture.

Motion and Momentum

Aikido is a very fluid and dynamic art. In the beginning, you will train by standing in a static position and practicing the techniques. Later, as your training partner approaches, you will begin to enter and blend with him by moving in to meet him and gently guiding or redirecting his momentum into the technique. Your technique will no longer be a sequential series of moves, but one fluid move. This fluidity of motion and momentum makes aikido look a lot like dance. Aikido is a very powerful dance of self-defense and personal transformation.

 Initially, you will practice your aikido techniques in a step-by-step sequence. Eventually, your technique will become one continuous fluid motion.

Move from Your Center

Your center of gravity is slightly below your navel. All movements are aligned with, and originate from, this center. Motion and momentum are initiated from the hip, coordinating all movement as one. An easy way to stay aware of your center is to keep thinking about moving your belt knot first. The knot of your belt, and eventually your hakama, will be placed directly over your center and can be used as a point of reference.

Become the Center

When doing circular movements, become the center of the circle, allowing your partner to rotate around you. O'Sensei Morihei Ueshiba believed that one should move like a beam of light, fly like lighting, strike like thunder, and whirl in circles around a stable center. Think of your center as the middle point of a circle. Think of your training partner's center as the middle of his or her circle. Standing at a distance from each other, you form an oval. As your training partner approaches or attacks, the distance between the centers lessens. Capturing the center, and becoming the center, leaves your training partner going around you on the periphery of the circle. A slight turn from the center will create a greater distance on the circumference of the circle. This circular motion makes use of both centripetal (inward spinning) and centrifugal (outward spinning) forces. Spin like a top. Hold your body straight and think of your turns as if you were a top spinning at the center of the circle. By becoming the center of the technique, you generate momentum and power.

Keep Your Training Partner Close

Do not let your training partner get too far away from you. To maintain control, keep very close contact. If you let your training partner get too far away from you, you will have to reach and overextend yourself beyond your balance point, breaking your own vertical physical alignment horizontally, and losing all your power. To maintain power in your technique, keep your circular movements tight and your training partner close.

Follow the Radius and Circumference

Aikido emphasizes circular movement, instead of movement in straight lines. There is less resistance on the radius of the circle, formed by the fully extended arm. Follow the radius along the circumference of the circular motion. The arms move most easily when allowed to follow the radius of this natural extension. There are circular lines of mobilization. By extending the arm's reach or radius slightly beyond full extension, your training partner will begin to lose balance and shift their priorities, mobilizing them to follow the direction you are leading them. Think of the path of your technique as being along a circle.

Move in One Continuous Motion

Instead of thinking or moving in steps, move as if the technique is one continuous motion, to maintain momentum and inertia. Maintain one continuous pull/tension from the initial contact to the completion of your technique. Once you have engaged or established contact with your partner, keep tension or pull in your technique. Keep one smooth rhythm. Blend with the pace of your partner. Do not speed up or jerk your technique. Do not let go or pull away too far or too fast. Try to keep your hand in constant continuous contact.

Unbalance Your Opponent

Many techniques allow you to unbalance the training partner with a whipping type of motion, by keeping your center and whipping your partner around you. By holding the head of your training partner or opponent against your center, you create centripetal force, keeping momentum pulled in. By allowing his feet to go around on the circumference of that circle, you create centrifugal force, causing the momentum of the feet to go farther out. The combination of centripetal and centrifugal force, while keeping your center in the circle, makes your training partner or opponent travel much faster than you. This causes your training partner to lose balance, making it easier to control and throw him.

When practicing, remember not to watch your hands. Keep your eyes focused on where you are leading the technique.

Another way to unbalance your training partner is to use a wave or dip type of motion. Many techniques work by dipping your partner down before raising and throwing him. This works especially well against taller partners. This wave effect works very well to disrupt and unbalance a training partner or opponent.

Focus As If No Obstacle or Resistance Is Present

Focus on your technique, not just your partner. Act as if your training partners are not there and you will move through them. The extension of your energy, or ki, stops where the focus of your mind stops. If your focus is on your training partner or opponent, your momentum and energy will stop there. By extending your vision though your training partner or opponent, you allow your energy to travel unimpeded. This works in the reverse for the approaching training partner or opponent, who expects his energy to stop at a certain point of contact. When you are no longer at that point, the energy stops or overextends, making it easier to move his limbs on the circumference of his range of motion, or to unbalance him.

Practice Slowly and Deliberately

Practice all techniques slowly, paying close attention to form before attempting to speed up. By practicing slowly, you actually learn the technique better, because you do not allow momentum alone to do the work. Slow motion facilitates the firing of the neural pathway that activates the muscles used. It also helps you use only the muscles and neurons needed, leaving the others relaxed, and preventing any wasted motion. When you use a light touch to redirect and match the speed of your training partner's or opponent's

There is some controversy in the use of strikes in aikido. Some feel that as a spiritual art, there is no room or need for strikes. Others feel that because aikido is a martial art, the strikes must be included. O'Sensei often used feints as the technique that would break his opponent's balance and send them flying.

approach, he feels his own motion, not yours, making your technique nearly invisible. Speed will come with consistent and persistent practice. Develop the technical skill, body awareness, and alignment first, then gradually practice at a faster pace.

Create an Empty Space

First, learn to empty the space you want your partner to occupy. He will fall into it because you have learned to take his balance, or because he is expecting you to be there to support him. Let him fall into the empty space you create. Another aspect of emptying is simply not being where your training partner expects you to be. When your training partner initiates an attack, he expects you to provide some resistance on impact. When the attack does not meet resistance, because you have moved and emptied that space, the attacker first becomes disoriented and loses mental balance, then becomes overextended and loses physical balance.

After you learn to empty the space, empty your mind from anticipating the approach and your response. The art of aikido is in allowing your training partner's approach and attack to dictate your technique.

Use Strikes and Feints (Atemi)

The use of strikes or feints distracts your training partner and interrupts his flow of energy, or ki. In many techniques the initial response includes a strike or feint to the face. This moves your training partner's attention from the technique to protect his face, leaving you with less resistance. A strike or feint to the face also causes the head to move backward to avoid the strike. This initial and often subtle movement becomes the beginning of taking the balance of your training partner. If he flinches backward, he takes his physical weight and mental attention backward, making him easier to throw backward. A lower strike or feint to the stomach or midsection will cause your training partner to lean forward, extending his physical weight and mental focus forward, and making him easier to throw in a forward direction. If you meet resistance in the application of a controlling technique, a slight strike or feint to the face will cause the opponent to stop concentrating or focusing on his

Some styles of aikido do not include yelling, or kiai. O'Sensei was known for being able to time his yells in such a way as to break his opponent's balance and send them flying without touching them.

hand and your motions. This frees that limb for the complete application of pinning and controlling.

Some Intangible Principles

Extend Your Ki

Ki is always important in aikido. You learn to feel the extension of your training partner's energy, or ki. You also become aware that your own energy extends beyond the limits of your technique. With each movement, exhale and extend your ki by imagining the energy extending past your body. Ki happens naturally when the body and mind unify.

Yell (*Kiai*)

A loud shout on execution can enhance your technique, forcing you to exhale, and it startles your training partner. It is your "spirit yell." O'Sensei Morihei Ueshiba would combine a loud kiai with timing, to cause his training partner to lose balance and throw himself, without being touched. As your training partner begins to move forward, before he has a chance to set his forward foot on the ground, his body leans without proper support or balance. If he is startled at this point, with precise timing, the startle response will interrupt his forward momentum and cause him to lose balance and fall. Many schools do not emphasize the usage of kiai in practice, for this reason.

Soft Eye Focus (*Metsuki*)

At first in aikido it is common to watch what you are doing. Many times, you will find your eyes on your hands. This is perfectly okay in the beginning. Later, as you gain proficiency and confidence in your techniques, it will become important to take your eyes off the technique itself. Keeping your eyes on your techniques leaves you open to other attacks, and telegraphs your intentions to your training partner. Some schools want you to look into the eyes of your training partner. You can see into his intentions this way, but he can also see into yours. Another option is to allow your eyes to look through or past your partner. This extends intent and makes it easier for you to spot motion off to the side. There is some evidence that this soft eye focus (*metsuki*) helps maintain a sense of emotional calm and detachment.

Training Tips

O'Sensei Morihei Ueshiba believed that one did not need buildings, money, power, or status to practice aikido. He believed that heaven was right where you are standing, and that is the place to train. Aikido training is not always safe, and if not done properly, it can be quite dangerous. In order to avoid serious injuries, you should adhere to certain rules. Never use muscle strength when applying a technique to your training partner. Be totally relaxed at all times, whether it is you or your partner who is doing the technique. Never counter your partner's technique by resisting. Always cooperate so you can help others progress. Aikido is not a martial art meant for fighting; therefore, never try to test each other's skills. Always review your old technique, because your new technique will derive from it.

Remember, we do not rise to the level of our expectations, but we do fall to the level of our training. So train well. O'Sensei Morihei Ueshiba believed that the purpose of training was to tighten up the slack, toughen the body, and polish the spirit.

It is said that we do not rise to the level of our expectations, but fall to the level of our expectations. Train well.

The basic principles of aikido are easy to put on paper. They are harder to understand. They are harder yet to apply to your aikido training. As you consistently and persistently practice, you will begin to feel and know these principles.

stances
and footwork

O' SENSEI MORIHEI UESHIBA would say that a good stance and posture (*kamae*) reflect a proper state of mind. The key to good techniques is to keep your hands, feet, and hips straight and centered. When centered, you can move freely. The physical center is your belly; if your mind is set there as well, victory is ensured in any endeavor.

The word *kamae* is the Japanese term used to describe "stances." The five main stances include *migi-hanmi*, stance with the right foot forward; *hidari-hanmi*, stance with the left foot forward; *ai-hanmi*, stance on the same side as your opponent; *gyaku-hanmi*, stance on the opposite side of your opponent; and no stance.

Basic Stances (*Kamae*)

In learning aikido, a lot of initial focus and emphasis is placed on the stance practice. The correct stance makes everything possible. It is a statement of the student's readiness to practice and to respond. The external posturing of the stance reflects the internal emotional and mental state of the student. A lot can be learned by studying the body language of various ready positions.

Stances, or postures, in aikido are called *kamae*. Another meaning for kamae is "attitude." The aikido stance extends to an inner attitude of peace and calm, although the body is poised and ready for action. Your posture and stance make a statement about your training. With your posture and stance, you face your opponent, your training partner, yourself, and the world.

There are five variations of the same aikido ready stance. The first two relate to yourself. You can have the right foot forward (*migi-hanmi*) or the left foot forward (*hidari-hanmi*). The second two are in relationship to your training partner: they are the *ai-hanmi*, or same side stance, and the *gyaku-hanmi*, or opposite side stance. The last stance is no stance: the body is simply relaxed and ready.

Figure 9-1: Ready stance

The Natural Ready Stance

First, let us look at the aikido natural ready stance. To get a feel for the naturalness of the aikido stance, simply take a comfortable easy step forward. The natural ready stance is not a separate stance. It is the way in which you hold yourself and the way you stand in relationship to your training partner. The posture of the natural ready stance prepares you to train, but does not provoke an aggressive or defensive response in your training partner. It is a natural way of standing that suggests you are ready.

Simply allow your body to settle until it is positioned, or centered and balanced, equally over the front and back legs. Do not lock your knees or overextend them so that your knees go beyond your toes. Keep the spine straight as if it were being pulled upward by a string attached to the middle (not front or back) of the head, helping to elongate and align the spine.

Turn the back foot to almost a ninety-degree angle, aligned and slightly behind the heel of the front foot, so that it forms a triangle. The foot positioning, as a triangle, provides an extremely stable, yet mobile, base of movement and power. Pushing off the back foot allows the strength of a movement to generate from the ground up, through the body, as opposed to just using the strength of the arms.

The body is kept in complete alignment by ensuring that the toes of the front foot, the knees, hips, chest, shoulders, chin, and eyes are all directed forward along the same centerline.

Allow the arms to rise along their natural radius of movement, with the elbows slightly bent, and rest them in front, about waist height. The hands are kept nonaggressively relaxed and open, ready for defense. If the hands are held open and relaxed, they give no clue as to the readiness to receive an attack. If the palms face slightly toward the attacker/training partner, they give the impression of submission and not wanting to fight. This nonoffensive positioning becomes a means to dissipate and de-escalate aggression. The body is held comfortably relaxed with normal breathing.

The eye focus, *metsuki*, is forward and looking at a distance. The soft focus held by the eyes in aikido allows the side vision to come into play. This improves your ability to see the opponent's entire body and detect motion faster. There is also some evidence that a strained hard focus creates tunnel vision and heightens emotion. The soft focusing—looking through, rather than at, the approaching training partner's eyes—allows you to maintain a detached, calm, relaxed readiness.

The Same Stance and the Opposite Stance

The two primary stances in aikido, taken in reference to the approaching training partner, are the same, or matching, stance (ai-hanmi) and the opposite, or reverse, stance (gyaku-hanmi).

In the ai-hanmi stance, both partners assume the same side stance with the same foot and hand forward. Notice the appropriate distance for the soft eye focus. Hands are held relaxed and in front of the body, aligning the centerline of your body with the centerline of your opponent or training partner.

In the gyaku-hanmi stance, the two partners assume opposite stances. Notice the appropriate distance for the soft eye focus. Hands are held relaxed and in front of the body, aligning the centerline of your body with the centerline of your opponent or training partner.

Figure 9-2: Ai-hanmi stance

Natural Stance

The natural neutral stance is actually no stance. It is the result of training your body to take the position and posture necessary for the situation. It is nonaggressive, but ready for action. The body is balanced by distributing your weight evenly between

Figure 9-3: Gyaku-hanmi stance

both feet. You are centered at your center of gravity, slightly below your navel. All movement originates from this area. You feel rooted as you become aware of your connection to the ground. Stay rooted with a firm foundation. Your strike is ready, and you are prepared to respond, not just react.

Your opponent's response when you do not make a strike is interesting. When you do not present either an aggressive or a defensive stance, there is no signal for your training partner to launch the approach or attack. When you take no stance and simply remain still, physically and mentally, you usually suspend all action.

> If you are having troubles with a technique, you may have the footwork wrong, as your footwork directs the movement and the flow of the technique.

Footwork (*Ashi-sabaki*)

There are only a few basic footwork patterns in aikido, called *ashi-sabaki*. They include the natural stepping forward, the shuffle, the cross-step, and the circular pivoting tenkan, which exemplifies the power and fluidity of aikido.

The Circular Pivoting Step (*Tenkan*)

Unique to aikido, the tenkan, or circular pivoting step, is the most powerful footwork (ashi-sabaki) pattern in the aikido repertory. It allows you to put your full weight and momentum into the technique. It consists of a simple step forward and then a swing of the back leg in a large circular C-shape pattern. It can be done forward or backward. By keeping your hands in front of you on your centerline, you can put your full body momentum into every move. The tenkan allows you to get off the line of attack and apply the principle of centrifugal and centripetal force to your technique.

The practice of the tenkan is crucial to developing power in aikido. Take a natural ready stance. Step forward and swing your back leg 180 degrees behind you, until you are facing the opposite direction. Step and turn again. Maintain your posture throughout this practice. If you have a training partner available, he or she can practice by facing you. Each of you step forward slightly off the line of attack, turn (tenkan), and continue to hold a soft-focus eye contact as you step to the opposite side. In essence, this exercise teaches you to change places with your attacker, opponent, or training partner. Used in application, the tenkan can put you directly behind an attacker, leaving you safe and leaving him very exposed to attack.

> The word *ashi-sabaki* is the Japanese term used to describe "footwork." The main footwork patterns include the *tenkan*, or circular pivoting step; *ayumi-ashi*, or the walking step; *tsugi-ashi*, or the shuffle step; and the cross-step.

The tenkan, or circular pivoting step, is unique to aikido and is the basis of generating momentum and power.

An interesting and effective training pattern combines a ninety-degree tenkan with a 180-degree tenkan. Assume a ready stance with your right foot forward. Keep your spine straight, head up, and all of your body parts aligned. Step forward with your left foot, keeping your hips, shoulders, and head level. Swing your right leg ninety degrees to your left in a circular pattern. Next, step forward, maintaining your posture. Swing your left leg 180 degrees in a circular pattern, until you are facing the opposite direction. Step forward with your left leg and swing your right leg in another ninety-degree circular pattern. You should now be facing directly into your original position. Take a step forward with your right leg, maintaining posture, and then swing the back leg in another 180-degree circular pattern. This will bring you back to your original position.

A slight variation of the above footwork pattern is to allow your hands to

Figure 9-4a: Tenkan start

Figure 9-4b: Tenkan transition

Figure 9-4c: Tenkan finish

hang loose, instead of holding them on your centerline. They will naturally swing out as you move. This footwork pattern helps you concentrate on initiating your movement from your hips or center. All movement in aikido should first come from this area. Staying centered is an extremely important principle in the practice of aikido.

Walking Step (*Ayumi-ashi*)

Ayumi-ashi means simply walking forward. Simply walking forward does not seem like a difficult task. Yet, when in a defensive situation, most people tend to lose their natural gait and overemphasize their movements. They tend to lunge rather than step. The practice of a walking step helps you to remain calm and move naturally. Assume the natural aikido stance as described earlier. Now simply walk. Make sure your movement originates from your hips and that you do not lean forward.

It is harder than most people think to simply walk and stay centered and balanced. Watch your reflection as you walk past a mirror or large picture window. Notice that you may lean too far forward and lead with your head rather than your body. You may become aware that there is a lot of up-and-down or side-to-side motion.

Some meditation styles require their practitioners maintain constant awareness, body relaxation, and mental calmness while walking. They count their steps, paying very close attention to their breath, movement, and surroundings in the present moment.

In ki development, you will learn to walk forward without any thought of your training partner. Your energy will stop where your focus or mental awareness stops. A common mental trick when breaking boards or bricks is to visualize *through* the obstacle and then to simply place the hand or foot on the imagined visualized target. This focus of awareness extends the energy or ki of the strike through the target, breaking it with ease. By just walking, you develop the ability to maintain a soft eye focus through your training partner, to maintain a calm mind and a relaxed body, and to extend ki even while in motion.

The Shuffle Step (*Tsugi–ashi*)

The shuffle step (*tsugi-ashi*) is like a fencer's lunge. To move forward, lead with the front foot, and bring the rear foot up behind it in an advancing or entering motion. To move backward, move the rear foot back and then shuffle the front foot back toward it. Remember to maintain your natural aikido ready stance, with your back straight, and move from your center or hip region.

The best way to think about and practice the shuffle step is in reference to the fencer's lunge. Assume a natural ready stance. Keep yourself centered and balanced. Lunge forward quickly with your front foot, bringing your rear foot close behind. Your feet stay on the same line.

Tsugi-ashi is often used to enter an attack. When your training partner approaches you, immediately move toward him or her with a quick lunge. The moving toward, not away from, the attack will take your training partners by surprise. You will have bridged the distance, intercepted their momentum, and possibly taken their balance before they have actually initiated their attack.

Used defensively, the shuffle step can allow you to move backward, blending with the attack, and staying out of range. Sometimes, this is a slight shuffle back to maintain a safe distance. A good practice drill is to respond to your training partner's tsugi-ashi movements. As your partner shuffles forward, you shuffle back. As your partner shuffles back, you shuffle forward. Every so often, for variety and surprise, shuffle forward slightly off-line, to intercept your partner's movement. Remember to trade places and let your partner learn to respond to you as you initiate the action.

Cross-Step

The cross-step is used to step across the centerline and position the body outside your training partner's striking range. It is not a common step in aikido. The cross-step is used as a transitional step to set up better positioning for a throw or locking technique.

Assume the basic natural ready aikido stance. As you step forward, instead of stepping directly forward, step so your leg crosses to the right, in front of your left leg, or vice versa.

Against a frontal attack, the cross-step transitions you from the inside to the outside of the attack, without giving up any ground. It is also used to respond when a stance change is appropriate or desired. The cross-step can be used as a shuffle step when you want to stay close to the body of your training partner. To enter, step by bringing your rear foot in front of you and then follow by sliding your other foot behind your training partner. This positioning alone can begin to intercept your training partner's momentum and interrupt his or her balance.

The word shikko is the Japanese term used to describe "knee-walking." Knee-walking helps to develop unification of body movement initiated from the center or hips. All techniques will eventually be executable from a kneeling position and all movement will be through tenkan, circular pivots, on the knees.

Knee-Walking (*Shikko*)

Shikko, or knee-walking, is unique to aikido. As you practice, you will learn to do all your techniques from a kneeling position (*suwari-waza*). In traditional Japanese culture, sitting on your heels in this kneeling position was common. Therefore, one had to learn to respond from this position.

Assume a kneeling (*seiza*) position with your back straight, body relaxed, and mind calm. Rise up from your hips. Lift your knees, moving forward. Keep your feet together and lower onto your forward knee. Use this knee as a pivot point to go from ai-hanmi to gyaku-hanmi stance, alternating which side of the body is forward. The pivoting is strictly from the hips and helps you learn to move from your center.

The stances (kamae) and footwork (ashi-sabaki) of aikido are the foundation on which you must build your techniques. Without a good stance, your foundation is weak. Without good footwork, there is no mobility.

chapter 10
strikes

SOME BELIEVE THAT the lack of actual striking in aikido makes it an incomplete art at best. O'Sensei Morihei Ueshiba chose to keep most of the strikes out of aikido, to make it a means for spiritual growth. However, some strikes have been adapted to aikido, for use in self-defense situations. When faced with conflict, aikido does not respond or react with force or violence.

Because aikido does not focus on strikes, aikido practitioners are often accused of not being able to strike at all. That is why it is very important for all practitioners to pay close attention to developing their striking abilities. This will provide your training partners with the opportunity to train against focused strikes that are intended to make contact with power.

The word atemi is the Japanese term used to describe "strikes." The main strikes in aikido are shomen-uchi, which means "front overhead downward strike"; yokomen-uchi, which means "front diagonal head or neck strike"; and tsuki, which means "front straight punch."

The Strikes (*Atemi*)

Aikido is not primarily a striking art, and beginner techniques are practiced by having the approaching training partner grab the wrists, as opposed to striking at them.

The three primary strikes or attacks that are practiced in aikido are the overhead strike, the diagonal head or neck strike, and the straight punch, which is usually aimed at the midsection. These are similar to the cutting motions used in the sword arts: straight down, downward at a forty-five-degree angle, and a thrusting of the blade. The execution of the overhead and diagonal strikes uses the hand blade, or side of the hand, much like a *shuto* in karate.

Front Overhead Downward Strike (*Shomen-uchi*)

First, bow to show respect to your opponent. Then establish a centered, balanced, neutral ready stance, at the appropriate distance, which is just out of striking range. Establish and maintain a soft eye focus through, not on, your training partner's eyes. Relax your breathing and your body. Calm your mind.

Raise your right or left hand directly overhead. If your right leg is forward, raise your right hand. If your left leg is forward, raise your left hand. Fan your fingers out and hold your hand as a hand blade. The striking surface would be the outside edge of your palm. The arm then becomes somewhat stiff as if it were a slightly curved spring. The arm moves as one unit, with the hand and fingers as a natural extension of the arm. Mimic the action of a sword cutting down, as if your hand blade were a sword blade. Step forward while simultaneously bringing the hand down. Make your movements committed and directly down your centerline. Use your training partner visually to sight or aim your strike from the top of his head directly down

Figure 10-1: Shomen-uchi

and through his centerline. The shomen-uchi should enter the body-line and continue through the centerline of the body. Perform a realistic and committed attack so your training partner can practice his defense. Keep your feet, hips, shoulders, and eyes aligned and aimed in the same direction as your strike. Keep your other hand in front of you, on your centerline, for protection. Exhale as you execute shomen-uchi.

Step back to the appropriate distance and bow to show respect.

The Front Diagonal Head or Neck Strike (*Yokomen-uchi*)

First, bow to show respect. Then establish a centered, balanced, neutral ready stance at the appropriate distance, just out of striking range. Establish and maintain a soft eye focus through, not on, your training partner's eyes. Relax your breathing and your body. Calm your mind.

Figure 10-2: Yokomen-uchi

Figure 10-3: Tsuki

Raise your hand blade overhead. Fan your fingers and hold them in a hand blade. The hand becomes aligned and a natural extension of your arm. Your arm is held stiff as a spring, with a slight curve or bend at the elbow. Do not lock the elbow. Imagine a forty-five-degree cut with a sword blade for your hand blade to follow. Bring your hand down at an angle toward the neck area, and follow through. As you execute the yokomen-uchi, step forward simultaneously with the same foot. Keep your other hand in front for protection. The diagonal path of the yokomen-uchi should continue, or follow through, to the centerline of the body. A yokomen-uchi can even cross the body's centerline to the far side of the body-line. If you pull short, not reaching into the body-line, you are not performing a legitimate committed attack, and therefore not giving your training partner the energy needed to practice aikido techniques. Exhale as you execute the yokomen-uchi. Step back to the appropriate distance and bow to show respect.

The Front Straight Punch or Thrust (*Tsuki*)

First, bow to show respect. Then establish a centered, balanced, neutral ready stance at the appropriate distance, just out of striking range. Establish and maintain a soft eye focus through your training partner's eyes. Relax your breathing and your body. Calm your mind.

Pull the hand on the same side as your rear leg back to your hip, with the palm up. (The right hand should be on the right hip if the right leg is back. The left hand should be on the left hip if the left leg is back.) Roll the fingers into a fist. Make sure your thumb is on the outside of your fingers and tucked along the side. If you place your thumb inside your fist, it will break on contact. As you step forward, simultaneously snap the fist out along your centerline, keeping your elbow down. Stepping at the same time as you strike allows you to bring your body weight and momentum into play, to produce more power than your arm could produce by itself. At the last moment, turn your fist over so the back of the hand is up. The first two knuckles should be in a direct line with the wrist, the elbow, and the shoulder. This puts the structural alignment and support directly behind your punch. The punch should stop at the center of your training partner. If you stop short of that target, you will not be giving your training partner a true attack to practice against. Keep your free hand in front for protection. Exhale as you execute mune-tsuki. There should be a snap at the end of your punch, much like the crack of a whip as it reaches full extension.

The best footwork for tsuki is a circle-C step. Stand in a ready stance, centered and balanced. There will be some space or distance between your feet. Make a circle-C step by bringing your back foot forward, into and alongside your front foot, and then back out as you continue to step forward. The punch should correspond exactly with the timing and placement of the front foot. The foot should touch the ground exactly at the same time as the punch reaches full extension and makes contact with the target.

A great way to practice punching is to walk the mat. This is a common training method in the striking arts. Step forward and punch. Step forward again and punch. Keep repeating the simultaneous step and punch, alternating sides, until you reach the end of the mat. Now turn around, step and punch all the way back.

To practice tsuki from a standing position, take a deep horse stance. A horse stance is established by placing your feet parallel and sitting back slightly as if seated on and straddling a horse. The horse stance is not commonly used in aikido and is only included in this section as a training tool. Punch with one hand and then the other. You can even practice double or triple punches, doing two or three each time, as fast and as powerfully as possible. You can vary the target. Punch to the head, the stomach, and the groin area. These are common targets in fighting.

Defensive Strikes or Feints (*Atemi*)

Atemi refers to defensive striking techniques. The aikidoka, or student of aikido, executes atemi to interrupt, or mislead, the attacker's forward momentum. The goal is not to do damage or harm. This would be against the nature of aikido. Strikes that do not actually make contact can be utilized as feints to distract or take the opponent's focus off the technique, thus "lightening the load," or reducing resistance. While entering, a quick jab toward the uke's eyes draws the attention upward. It also causes the body to move away from the atemi and unbalances the uke. If you encounter resistance, you can easily reduce it by making an atemi, or feint, toward the eyes and then immediately applying the technique. All vulnerable targets of the body are good choices for targets of atemi, since they draw the uke's immediate attention.

It is said that O'Sensei Morihei Ueshiba eventually used atemi or feints exclusively to throw opponents. He simply timed his atemi precisely at a point of unbalance in the opponent's approach or attack, which would cause them to lose their balance completely and throw themselves to the ground.

The word geri is the Japanese term used to describe "kicks." Very few kicking techniques or defenses are practiced in aikido.

Kicks (*Geri*)

Aikido does not teach kicks, or *geri*, in the formal sense. Kicks take balance to execute, they telegraph your intentions, and they are the easiest attacks to defend against. However, in advanced stages of training, many practitioners like to apply the principles of aikido, primarily blending and taking of balance, to defend against kicks. The principles apply equally well to kicks as to any strikes, but kicks require more attention to distance. The practice of aikido against kicks takes confidence and timing, and is usually reserved for more advanced training.

Since aikido does not teach defense against kicking techniques until a very advanced level, there is no need to explain the actual execution of the front, side, or roundhouse kick here. These kicks follow much the same angles of attack as described for the strikes. When you reach the level at which you want to execute and defend against kicks, please get competent instruction.

The use of strikes in aikido cannot be overemphasized. First, the ability to deliver strikes competently, with commitment and power, will allow your training partners to get the most from their training. It will also allow you to train persistently and consistently against them.

As you become familiar with the angles of an attack, you will begin to understand and perceive that any hand, elbow, knee, or foot strike, following these angles, can be handled with the same aikido techniques. You will learn to use your footwork to enter and blend with these lines and angles of attack. That also applies to any weapon that follows these angles of attack. Should the need arise, atemi at full force can be used in self-defense situations. This subject will be covered later.

chapter 11
grabs

ONE OF THE FIRST THINGS beginners of aikido notice is that they are practicing their techniques by letting someone grab them. This is foreign to most people. Why would you ever let someone grab you? It just doesn't seem safe. It isn't safe. But if you can learn to make aikido work when someone grabs you, your technique will be even more effective when you're not at this disadvantage.

Grabs are unusual encounters in martial arts training. Other than the grappling arts, most martial arts teach strikes and kicks rather than grabs. There are several reasons why aikido emphasizes the application of grabs: First, grabs do happen more often than people want to admit. Second, grabs make it easier to learn the sensitivity needed for the proper application of aikido techniques.

The Grabs of Aikido

There are four basic wrist grabs in aikido. They are grabbing the same wrist (ai-hanmi), grabbing the opposite wrist (gyaku- hanmi), grabbing both wrists with both hands (*ryote-dori*), and grabbing one wrist with two hands (*morote-dori*).

Always grab simultaneously with stepping forward. You will notice that advanced practitioners of aikido tend to grab and hold using the thumb and last three fingers. To execute a grab, point the first finger in the direction of motion. This helps to direct the mind of both training partners and the ki, or energy, flow. Keep your body aligned so that your feet, knees, hips, shoulders, and eyes are all aimed directly at your training partner's centerline. Keep your wrist straight and aligned with your elbow and shoulders. Keep your elbow down and your hand in front of your body at all times. Breathe in as you prepare to move, and exhale as you move forward and grab.

The word *dori* is the Japanese term used to describe "grabs." The four basic wrist grabs are ai-hanmi, which is grabbing the same wrist; *gyaku-hanmi*, which is grabbing the opposite wrist; *ryote-dori*, which is grabbing both wrists with both hands; *morote-dori*, which is grabbing one wrist with two hands.

All grabs are practiced with both the right and left hand. While many people favor one side, aikido training creates a sense of skillful ambidexterity. You are not doing yourself any favors by avoiding what you need to learn and practice. Eventually, when testing for a belt promotion, what you have practiced and what you have avoided will be obvious.

Initially, in aikido, these grabs are taught from a stationary position. In other words, one training partner stands and extends a hand, and the other training partner grabs as instructed. As the grab comes in, you will blend with the incoming momentum by stepping off the line and making a circular tenkan step to the front or back.

It is important to learn the basic grabs of aikido because, as you progress, the first part of your instruction will be which grab, or strike, you are to be attacked with. The instructions will then specify which throw or wrist-lock to follow up with, and whether to do it to your training partner's front or back. Sound complicated? It is at first. Be patient.

11-1: Ai-hanmi grab

The Same, or Matching (*Ai-hanmi*), Grab

The ai-hanmi grab, like the ai-hanmi stance, is executed right hand to right hand or left hand to left hand. To execute this grab, the training partner reaches across the body's centerline.

First, bow to show respect. Then establish a centered, balanced, neutral ready stance at the appropriate distance, just out of striking range. Establish and maintain a soft eye focus through your training partner's eyes. Relax your breathing and your body. Calm your mind.

Enter by stepping forward. Reach across your centerline and grab your training partner's opposite wrist. You will be grabbing the right wrist with your right hand, or the left wrist with your left hand. Do not turn your body to the side. Your feet, knees, hips, shoulders, and eyes should all be aligned and facing forward directly into your training partner's centerline. At first, your grab should be somewhat weak. This is to allow your training partner the opportunity to practice a throwing or locking technique. Too much resistance too soon interrupts training progress. Eventually you will want to extend the force of your grab through the forward direction of your grab, and the forward momentum of your body will be projected and extended. You will also use the power of your ki in grabbing. The grab uses the grip of the hand, not the muscles of the arm. This feels somewhat strange at first, as you are holding on tightly without using your arm strength.

Let go and move away to the appropriate distance, just out of striking distance. Keep the soft eye focus, maintaining a lingering focus or concentration between yourself and the training partner after the completion of all techniques. Maintain an awareness of your environment, as if sensing, and being ready for, the next attack. Bow to show respect.

Figure 11-2: Gyaku-hanmi grab

The Opposite, or Reverse (Gyaku-hanmi), Grab

The gyaku-hanmi grab is like the gyaku-hanmi stance. The right hand will grab the left, or the left hand will grab the right. Thus, the grab is executed on the same side, with the training partners facing each other.

First, bow to show respect. Then establish a centered, balanced, neutral ready stance at the appropriate distance, just out of striking range. Establish and maintain a soft eye focus through your training partner's eyes. Relax your breathing and your body. Calm your mind.

Enter by stepping forward. Reach out for your opponent's hand—grabbing the left wrist with your right hand, or the right wrist with your left hand. Keep your elbow down and your wrist straight. Keep your feet, knees, hips, shoulders, and eyes aligned and aimed straight at your training partner's centerline. Project your body momentum and ki energy forward. Hold with your hand, not your arm, and hold with your thumb and last three fingers, with your index finger pointing and free. Exhale as you grab.

Let go and move away to the appropriate distance, just out of striking range. Keep the soft eye focus, maintaining a lingering focus or concentration between yourself and your training partner after the completion of all techniques. Maintain an awareness of your environment, as if sensing, and being ready for, the next attack. Bow to show respect.

Two Hands Grab Two Wrists (*Ryote-dori*)

First, bow to show respect. Then establish a centered, balanced, neutral ready stance at the appropriate distance, just out of striking range. Establish and maintain a soft eye focus through your training partner's eyes. Relax your breathing and your body. Calm your mind.

Enter by simultaneously stepping forward and grabbing both your training partner's wrists with both your hands—grabbing his left wrist with your right hand and his right wrist with your left hand. Keep your feet, knees, hips, shoulders, and eyes aligned and aimed straight through your training partner's centerline. Use your thumb and last three fingers to grab, and your index finger to point. Hold with your hands, not your arms. Keep your elbows down. Exhale as you grab.

Let go and move away to the appropriate distance, just out of striking distance. Keep the soft eye

Figure 11-3: Ryote-dori grab

focus, maintaining a lingering focus or concentration between yourself and your training partner after the completion of all techniques. Maintain an awareness of your environment, as if sensing, and being ready for, the next attack. Bow to show respect.

Two Hands Grab One Wrist (*Morote-dori*)

First, bow to show respect. Then establish a centered, balanced, neutral ready stance at the appropriate distance, just out of striking range. Establish and maintain a soft eye focus through your training partner's eyes. Relax your breathing and your body. Calm your mind.

Enter by stepping forward. Grab one of your training partner's wrists with

Figure 11-4: Morote-dori grab

both of your hands—your right and left hand will grab his right or left wrist. Step and grab as one motion. Keep your wrist aligned with your elbow and shoulder. Keep your feet, knees, hips, shoulders, and eyes focused and aimed at your training partner's centerline. Hold with your hands, not your arms. Hold with your thumb and last three fingers, using your index finger to point. Exhale as you grab.

Let go and move away to the appropriate distance, just out of striking distance. Keep the soft eye focus, maintaining a lingering concentration between yourself and your training partner after the completion of all techniques. Maintain an awareness of your environment, as if sensing, and being ready for, the next attack. Bow to show respect.

Advanced Grabs in Aikido

Aikido teaches you to be able to respond to almost any type of grab. Each technique has an application. Some of the more advanced grabs include sleeve (*sode-dori*), collar (*eri-dori*), elbow (*hiji-dori*), shoulder (*kata-dori*), lapel (*muna-dori*), and both shoulders (*ryo-kata-dori*) grabs. Front grabs can also be combined with a strike, such as grabbing the lapel (muna-dori) with one hand and pulling your training partner into a strike (tsuki).

All of these grabs can be applied from the back (ushiro), and are often combined with a choke.

Grabs are very important in aikido training. At first, most of your training in techniques will work from a grab. This is easier for you to learn and helps you to develop an actual feel for the technique. Grabs also actually do happen—many people actually do get grabbed when attacked. Learn to grab effectively to help your training partner develop effective and powerful executions. Learn to respond appropriately to different grabs when you receive them. Learn mentally to grab the concepts of aikido and never let them go.

chapter 12
throwing
techniques

WHEN ONE FIRST SEES the graceful fluid movements of aikido, it is easy to question its effectiveness. It would appear that the partners are cooperating with each other rather than fighting each other. The basic techniques of aikido look easy and effortless. With a simple movement, an attacker is flying through the air. As a skilled aikidoka begins to enter and blend with his training partner's techniques, the demonstration can take on the appearance of a well-rehearsed, choreographed dance. When the *tori* (the one practicing the technique) feels any resistance from the uke (the one attacking and probably taking the fall), they move into another technique. One technique flows into another as dictated by the attacker. Once off balance, the uke is thrown effortlessly to the floor. Sound easy? To an experienced aikidoka it is—it just takes years of practice.

The Basic Throwing Techniques (*Nage-waza*)

There is no fixed number of techniques, only infinite possibilities. Aikido always takes into account the situation and opponent, thus keeping the art spontaneous.

Beginners to aikido learn various *nage*, or throwing techniques. These include *shiho-nage* (four-corner throw), *kote-gaeshi-nage* (wrist out-turning throw), *irimi-nage* (entering throw), *kaiten-nage* (rotary throw), and *tenbin-nage* (elbow-lock throw). Aikido has an infinite number of *kokyu-nage* (breathing and timing throws), such as the *tenchi-nage* (heaven and earth throw). Some consider all aikido techniques kokyu-nage. Kokyu-nage look like the easiest techniques, but they are the hardest to master. Kokyu-nage demonstrate and illustrate the basic principles of aikido and require you to develop your sensitivity and flow, allowing your training partner to hold on throughout the execution of the throw. Kokyu-nage work through movement, momentum, and the effective and proficient application of the throw.

Falls and Rolls (*Ukemi*)

It is impossible to learn aikido without learning how to fall and roll. There are several ukemi, or falling ways, that must be learned before being able to train and take the fall. You will learn to fall and roll forward or backward, as well as to the side. When you first begin to practices falls, you will find that you have a lot of edges. You may even roll more like a box than a ball. As you practice, you will begin to take the edges off and roll more like a ball.

Figure 12-1: Forward roll

Forward Roll and Fall (*Mae-ukemi*)

Aikido stresses that the most important thing for beginners to learn is the joy and benefit of ukemi, the falling techniques. Without the ability to take throws, it is impossible to practice aikido. Aikido emphasizes that the student should stay relaxed in the body and calm in the mind while practicing. It is important for the uke (the one receiving the technique) to learn to relax and exhale on the falls (ukemi). Training partners, staying relaxed and moving slowly, develop a sense of safety, trust, and mutual respect. The training strives for this harmony.

You will probably spend most of your first classes learning the front roll and the break-fall. They are essential to practicing, since you will be alternating as training partners, allowing both persons to practice and train in the techniques.

The front roll starts from a kneeling or standing position. If your right foot is forward, reach down with your right hand. If your left foot is forward, reach down with your left hand. Place your little finger just in front of your toes, with the fingers pointing back toward you. Place your other hand palm-down, fingers forward, on the mat next to the hand in front of your toes. Rock back and forth a few times by pushing slightly with the back leg. Allow your arms to feel like a rounded spring. Keep a circular image in your mind. Relax the body. Gently push off the back leg and roll up the arm, pulling the chin in slightly to protect it, over the shoulder, diagonally across the back, and up the opposite

> The word *ukemi* is the Japanese word used to describe "falls." The main falls include *mae-ukemi*, which means "forward roll and fall"; *ushiro-ukemi*, which means "backward roll and fall"; *ushiro-hanten-ukemi*, which means "backward and forward rolling"; *yoko-ukemi*, which means "side fall."

hip, and then let momentum take you to your original position. This is not the same as a front somersault, which takes you directly over your head and straight down your back. Protect and support your head at all times by keeping it slightly tucked in. Exhale as you roll.

Once you get the general idea of front rolls, begin to practice them as a continuous series of rolls, and finally as alternating rolls.

The front break-fall is very similar to the front roll. This time, instead of allowing momentum to return you to your starting position, just allow the

Figure 12-2: Side and forward fall

legs to lie out straight so you land flat on the mat. You will be slightly on your side. Bend the top leg so that the foot lands flat on the mat behind the bottom outstretched leg. As you land, the bottom hand slaps the mat to help absorb the impact. Exhale as you land.

Advanced practitioners will begin to take the rolls and break-falls with only the support of the front arm, held as a round spring. Even greater skill is needed to take the break-fall. This shows the true art of being a good training partner. It will eventually become easier for you to take the fall than to run the risk of pain and injury by not cooperating with the technique.

A combination of the roll and the break-fall is accomplished by initiating the roll, then slapping the mat at the bottom of the roll, as in the break-fall. Use the energy or momentum of the slap to propel yourself further into a standing position. Exhale as you roll.

Figure 12-3: Backward roll

Backward Roll and Fall (*Ushiro-ukemi*)

The backward roll is initiated from a one-knee position. The back leg is positioned by laying the shin on the mat directly below the body. The front leg is positioned with the knee up and the foot flat on the mat. The back leg and front foot form a solid triangular foundation. If the right leg is the back leg, extend the right arm to the side. If the left leg is the back leg, extend the left arm to the side. Place the other hand next to the head, with the fingers pointed toward the shoulder and the palm aligned with the top of your head. Exhale and keep the image of a circle in mind as you begin the backward roll. First, sit down over your back leg. Allow the momentum to carry you over your hip and diagonally across your back. Do not roll on the top of your head, as in a backward somersault. The head turns to the side and is protected by the arms. Finish by aiding your momentum by pushing your body up with your supporting hand.

To turn the back roll into a break-fall, just allow your body to roll backward, and slap the mat. The slapping absorbs the impact and stops the momentum.

Once you have mastered the backward roll from a kneeling position, start practicing taking the roll from a standing position. Advanced practitioners can throw their bodies backward and take the break-fall.

Backward and Forward Rolling (*Ushiro-hanten-ukemi*)

A combination of backward and forward motion allows your training partner to stay in eye contact with you. After first taking a backward roll, he can use the momentum to rebound into a forward roll and strike when his back touches the ground.

Figure 12-4: Backward fall

Side Fall (Yoko-ukemi)

The side fall begins in a standing position. Lift and swing up the leg and arm on the same side, to the point at which you begin to lose balance. Rather than attempting to catch yourself, let yourself fall. Just as you touch the ground, slap the mat with your hand to help absorb the impact. The hand, the side of the body, and the side of the leg should all hit at the same time. Stay relaxed and exhale as you land. The landing of the side fall will look just like the forward fall.

Standing Throwing Techniques (Tachi-Nage)

All techniques will be practiced or executed in response to all possible approaches: a grab with the same hand executed to the front (*ai-hanmi omote*), a grab with the same hand executed to the rear (*ai-hanmi ura*), a grab with the opposite hand executed to the front (*gyaku-hanmi omote*), a grab with the opposite hand executed to the rear (*gyaku-hanmi ura*), two hands grabbing two wrists executed to the front (*ryote-dori omote*), two hand grabbing two wrists executed to the rear (*ryote-dori ura*), two hands grabbing one wrist executed to the front (*morote-dori omote*), two hands grabbing one wrist executed to the

Aikido throws follow a sequence: (1) enter and blend, (2) redirect and break balance, (3) throw or control, and (4) let go and move away.

rear (*morote-dori ura*), an overhead strike executed to the front (*shomen-uchi omote*), an overhead strike executed to the rear (*shomen-uchi ura*), a diagonal strike executed to the front (*yokomen-uchi omote*), a diagonal strike executed to the rear (*yokomen-uchi ura*), and a midsection punch or thrust executed to the front (*tsuki omote*).

Entering Throw (Irimi-nage)

Irimi, or entering, is a basic throw in aikido. It takes the application of all the aikido principles to make it powerful and effective. Its looks deceptively simple.

Entering Throw against an Overhead Strike (Shomen-uchi Irimi-nage)

First, bow to show respect. Then establish a centered, balanced, neutral ready stance at the appropriate distance, just out of striking range. Establish and maintain a soft eye focus through your training partner's eyes. Relax your breathing and your body. Calm your mind.

When your training partner attempts to strike down to your face, quickly step in with your left foot. Perform irimi-nage by cutting down with your hand blade while pivoting widely or simply stepping through and behind your training partner to break his balance.

Your training partner approaches and attacks with a downward overhead strike (shomen-uchi). You enter and blend by shuffling forward just off the at-

Figure 12-5a: Shomen-uchi irimi-nage, first part

tack line. Inhale as you enter and blend. As your one hand intercepts and deflects the attacking arm at the elbow, your other hand strikes to the rib cage (see Figure 12-5a), causing your training partner to bend forward and begin to lose balance. Raise your striking hand to your training partner's elbow and slide the other one to his wrist. Step forward, toward his hip, as you pivot, or tenkan, behind him (see Figure 12-5b). Blend and redirect by swinging him with your full body momentum. As he

Figure 12-5b: Shomen-uchi irimi-nage, second part

Figure 12-5c: Shomen-uchi irimi-nage, third part

follows your redirection, intercept his momentum by raising your hand to the side of his head, placing your forearm along his jaw line from chin to ear (see Figure 12-5c). Pull him close to your body. Take his balance and throw him by letting his body momentum carry his legs in one direction while you project his head the other way. This throws him. Maintain control throughout the technique, guiding him to a safe landing. Exhale as you throw.

Let go and move away to the appropriate distance, just out of striking distance. Keep the soft eye focus, maintaining a lingering focus or concentration between yourself and your training partner after the completion of all techniques. Maintain an awareness of your environment, as if sensing, and being ready for, the next attack. Bow to show respect.

Variations of the Entering Throw (Henka-waza Irimi-nage)

There are many variations (*henka-waza*) of irimi-nage. Irimi-nage is basic to aikido and is said to be the thirty-year technique, since it will take you thirty years to master all the subtleties of it.

Entering Throw to the Rear against a Same-Hand Grab (Ai-hanmi Irimi-nage Ura)

When your training partner grabs your right hand with his right hand, take a big step in with your left foot. Move in to the side with a circular motion, while cutting down with the hand blade to break his balance. Maintain control, step in, and then cut down with the hand blade.

Entering Throw to the Rear against an Opposite-Hand Grab
(*Gyaku-hanmi Irimi-nage Ura*)

As your partner steps in and grabs you with the opposite hand (gyaku-hanmi), slide your front foot forward and outside his front foot. Following the natural extension or circular radius, raise his arm up toward his face. As you step through, allow your forearm to come across your partner's jaw. Continue to step through as if naturally walking, bringing your hand directly down your partner's back. The other hand pushes the lower back through, causing more imbalances.

Rotary Throw against a Straight Punch
(*Tsuki Kaiten-nage*)

To defend against a forward straight punch, a rotary throw is an excellent choice. You quickly get off the line of attack, defend yourself, take your training partner's balance, and throw him in one fluid step. Kaiten-nage is difficult to master in both execution and receiving. Train slowly and carefully.

First, bow to show respect. Then establish a centered, balanced, neutral ready stance at the appropriate distance, just out of striking range. Establish and maintain a soft eye focus through your training partner's eyes. Relax your breathing and your body. Calm your mind.

Your training partner approaches and attacks with a straightforward punch (tsuki). You enter by shuffling forward off the attack line. Allow the strike to

Figure 12-6a: Tsuki kaiten-nage, first part

Figure 12-6b: Tsuki kaiten-nage, second part

Figure 12-6c: Tsuki kaiten-nage, third part

continue to its full extension. The lack of anticipated contact and resistance will initially cause your training partner to lose balance, physically and mentally. Enter, blend with, and redirect the attack by intercepting the attacking hand and arm at the same horizontal level at which the attack is delivered. Slide your intercepting hand from the elbow down to his wrist as you begin to guide the arm downward, following its natural radius (see Figure 12-6a). Inhale as you enter and blend. Pull his arm all the way back and pull his head into your center (see Figure 12-6b). Follow the circular motion and push forward, across his body, while twisting at the waist and projecting your ki to throw your training partner (see Figure 12-6c). Exhale as you throw.

Let go and move away to the appropriate distance, just out of striking distance. Keep the soft eye focus, maintaining a lingering focus or concentration between yourself and your training partner after the completion of all techniques. Maintain an awareness of your environment, as if sensing, and being ready for, the next attack. Bow to show respect.

Variation of the Rotary Throw (*Henka–waza Kaiten-nage*)
Rotary Throw to the Front against a Same-Hand Grab (*Ai–hanmi Kaiten-nage Omote*)

As your partner steps in and grabs you with the ai-hanmi grab (see Figure 11-1), slide your front foot forward and just outside his front foot. Blend with the forward momentum, following the circular radius motion to bring your partner's hand downward and back with your forward hand. Placing your other hand on your partner's neck, pull him against you as you continue to bring his arm back. Step through and forward as you push his back arm diagonally across his body and throw him forward.

A Wrist Turn-Out Throw against a Diagonal Strike (*Yokomen-uchi Kote-gaeshi*)

Yokomen-uchi is the diagonal side strike with the hand blade, or shuto ridge of the hand, aimed diagonally at the head or neck. The application of the wrist

Figure 12-7a: Yokomen-uchi kote-gaeshi, first part

turn-out throw (kote-gaeshi) is a natural means to blend, take balance, and throw. Practice slowly to get the timing of the catch. Practice carefully, since any quick movement or application of too much strength can cause severe pain and injury to the wrist.

First, bow to show respect. Then establish a centered, balanced, neutral ready stance at the appropriate distance, just out of striking range. Establish and maintain a soft eye focus through your training partner's eyes. Relax your breathing and your body. Calm your mind.

Your training partner approaches and attacks with a downward diagonal strike (yokomen-uchi) toward the side of your head or neck. Enter by stepping in and intercepting the attacking arm (see Figure 12-7a). Inhale as you enter and blend. Blend and redirect the strike by following its line of attack and

Figure 12-7b: Yokomen-uchi kote-gaeshi, second part

shuffling into the attacker's center (see Figure 12-7b). Pivoting at your center, or hip, twist the wrist out, causing your training partner to lose balance and

Figure 12-7c: Yokomen-uchi kote-gaeshi, third part

change his priority from counterstriking to protecting his skeletal system from injury. Your redirection and taking of his balance will throw him over his own wrist (see Figure 12-7c). Exhale as you throw.

Let go and move away to the appropriate distance, just out of striking distance. Keep the soft eye focus, maintaining a lingering focus or concentration between yourself and your training partner after the completion of all techniques. Maintain an awareness of your environment, as if sensing, and being ready for, the next attack. Bow to show respect.

Variations of the Wrist Turn-Out Throw (Henka-waza Kote-gaeshi)
A Wrist Turn-Out Throw to the Rear against a Same-Hand Grab (Ai-hanmi Kote-gaeshi Omote)

As your partner steps forward, grabbing you with an ai-hanmi grab, step out to his front, swinging your palm up. Grab his wrist with your other hand and turn out. As you step back, continue turning his wrist by applying pressure with your hand blade to the back of his wrist, and throw him.

Wrist Turn-Out Throw to the Rear against an Opposite-Hand Grab (Ai-hanmi Kote-gaeshi Ura)

As your partner steps forward and grabs, ai-hanmi, slide your forward foot up and outside his. At the same time, swing your hand, palm up, to shoulder height. Place your other hand on the back of your partner, turning the wrist out. Step forward and behind (ura) your training partner, applying hand blade pressure on the back of his wrist, then throw him backward.

Four-Direction Throw against a Double-Hand Grab (*Ryote-dori Shiho-nage*)

First, bow to show respect. Then establish a centered, balanced, neutral ready stance at the appropriate distance, just out of striking range. Establish and maintain a soft eye focus through your training partner's eyes. Relax your breathing and your body. Calm your mind.

Figure 12-8a: Ryote-dori shiho-nage, first part

Your training partner approaches and grabs both of your wrists, the ryote-dori grab (see Figure 12-8a). Just before he makes contact, enter and redirect the attack across your centerlines (see Figure 12-8b). Inhale as you enter and blend. Continue to follow the momentum and lift up from underneath his elbow, raising him onto his toes and taking his balance. Step through and pivot. Keep following the circular arc of the arm until his hand is tucked directly behind his head and pointing toward his heels. The head should be behind the heels so that your training partner keeps his priority on his balance rather than counterstriking or attacking you (see Figure 12-8c). Follow the circular motion of the hands to throw your training partner. Exhale as you throw.

Figure 12-8b: Ryote-dori shiho-nage, second part

Let go and move away to the appropriate distance, just out of striking distance. Keep the soft eye focus, maintaining a lingering focus or concentration between yourself and your training partner after the completion of all techniques. Maintain an awareness of your environment, as if sensing, and being ready for, the next attack. Bow to show respect.

Variations of the Four-Direction Throw (Henka-waza Shiho-nage)

The Four-Direction Throw to the Front against a Same-Hand Grab (Ai-hanmi Shiho-nage Omote)

Figure 12-8c: Ryote-dori shiho-nage, third part

As your partner steps in and grabs you with the same hand (ai-hanmi), meet his wrist with an extended arm, palm down, pushing it to his front (omote) as you cross-step. Grab your partner's wrist with both of your hands. Placing your elbow under your partner's, raise up your elbow so that you lift your training partner onto his toes and take his balance. Continue to step through, turning at the hips, following the wrist upward on a vertical circle and keeping your hands slightly in front. Throw in the direction he was going.

The Four-Direction Throw to the Rear against a Same-Hand Grab (Ai-hanmi Shiho-nage Ura)

As your training partner comes in and grabs you with the same hand (ai-hanmi), slide your foot forward and just to the outside of your partner's. Grab his wrist with both your hands. Execute a pivot turn (tenkan) to his rear (ura). Follow his hands overhead on a vertical circle with hands slightly in front. Throw your partner back (ura) in the direction he was coming from.

The Four-Direction Throw against an Opposite-Hand Grab (Gyaku-hanmi Katate-dori Shiho-nage Omote)

When your training partner grabs your right wrist with his left hand, grab his left hand with your left hand and step forward to the front. Swing your hands up. Pivot to the left, and cut down with the hand blade while holding his arm.

There are four things you can do in this situation. You can throw in all four directions, which is how shiho-nage got its name. First, as your training partner steps in and grabs your wrist in an ai-hanmi grab, follow the steps above for omote. Instead of stepping in deeply in front of your partner, stay slightly in front of him. Turn and throw ninety degrees to the side, rather than straight forward. Second, following the ura steps above, step through very deeply to clear the body, and throw ninety degrees to the side, rather than straight back. Third, follow the steps for shiho-nage ura, as described before. Last, the fourth direction follows the directions given for shiho-nage omote, explained previously.

Figure 12-9a: , Morote-dori tenbin-nage, first part

Figure 12-9b: , Morote-dori tenbin-nage, second part

The Elbow-Lock Throw against a Double-Hand Grab to One Wrist (*Morote-dori Tenbin-nage*)

First, bow to show respect. Then establish a centered, balanced, neutral ready stance at the appropriate distance, just out of striking range. Establish and maintain a soft eye focus through your training partner's eyes. Relax your breathing and your body. Calm your mind.

Your training partner approaches and grabs one of your wrists with both of his hands (morote-dori). See Figure 12-9a. You enter and blend by flowing back with his momentum, sliding slightly off the attack line. Inhale as you enter and blend. Pull slightly to help take his balance (see Figure 12-9b). Reach with a hand blade inside his wrist while you grab his wrist from underneath. Redi-

Figure 12-9c: , Morote-dori tenbin-nage, third part

rect his momentum by swinging him back in the direction he came from. Rotate the hand over and then under his arm. Holding your hand palm up, lift slightly on his elbow to take his balance and change his priority from attack to compliance. As you step forward into his hip, project your arm forward and turn the palm over. Continue to follow through on the throw to control your training partner (see Figure 12-9c). Exhale as you throw.

Let go and move away to the appropriate distance, just out of striking distance. Keep the soft eye focus, maintaining a lingering focus or concentration between yourself and your training partner after the completion of all techniques. Maintain an awareness of your environment, as if sensing, and being ready for, the next attack. Bow to show respect.

Variation of the Elbow-Lock Throw (Henka-waza Tenbin-nage)
The Elbow-Lock Throw to the Front against an Opposite-Hand Grab (Gyaku-hanmi Tenbin-nage Omote)

As your partner steps in to grab you with his opposite hand (gyaku-hanmi), step out and to his front (omote) as you turn his wrist upward following the natural circular radius of his momentum. As you step through with your back leg, bring your forearm up, palm up, under his elbow pushing it up and forward. Throw your partner by turning your palm over and continuing to push forward and down.

Breath and Timing Throws (Kokyu-nage)

Kokyu-nage, or breath and timing throws, look the simplest, yet are the most difficult techniques in aikido. They depend on the proper execution of aikido principles. The entering and blending alone in these techniques allow you to take your training partner's balance and throw him or her effortlessly.

A Breath Throw against a Same-Hand Grab (*Gyaku-hanmi Kokyu-nage*), #1

First, bow to show respect. Then establish a centered, balanced, neutral ready stance at the appropriate distance, just out of striking range. Establish and maintain a soft eye focus through your training partner's eyes. Relax your breathing and your body. Calm your mind.

Figure 12-10a: Gyaku-hanmi kokyu-nage #1, first part

Your training partner approaches and grabs your wrist with the same hand (gyaku-hanmi). Just before contact is made, enter and blend forward to meet his approaching hand. Inhale as you enter and blend, and immediately redirect his momentum by swinging your hand out to the side and pointing back toward his balance point, which is a shin's length directly back from his centerline (see Figure 12-10a). Extend your arm behind your training partner until you have taken his balance, and throw him (see Figure 12-10b). Exhale as you throw. Continue to extend your ki and maintain a lingering focus (*zanshin*).

Let go and move away to the appropriate distance, just out of striking distance. Keep the soft eye focus, maintaining a lingering focus or concentration between yourself and your training partner after the completion of all techniques. Maintain an awareness of your environment, as if sensing, and being ready for, the next attack. Bow to show respect.

Figure 12-10b: Gyaku-hanmi kokyu-nage #1, second part

A Breath Throw against a Same-Hand Grab (Gyaku-hanmi Kokyu-nage), #2

First, bow to show respect. Then establish a centered, balanced, neutral ready stance at the appropriate distance, just out of striking range. Establish and maintain a soft eye focus through your training partner's eyes. Relax your breathing and your body. Calm your mind.

Figure 12-11a: Gyaku-hanmi kokyu-nage #2, first part

Figure 12-11b: Gyaku-hanmi kokyu-nage #2, second part

Your training partner approaches and grabs your wrist with the same hand (gyaku-hanmi). Immediately inhale as you enter and blend by stepping in and slightly off the attack-line. As you move in and to the side, gently redirect the attack by raising your hand, following the natural radius arc of his arm. Continue following the natural radius arc upward until his hand is behind his head and his elbow is pointing upward (see Figure 12-11a). His head will be beyond the balance line of his heels, and that will take your training partner's balance and change his priority, or focus of attention, to trying not to fall. Pulling his hand down the back while projecting his elbow on a circular path will make the throw easier (see Figure 12-11b). Exhale as you throw. Continue to follow through the momentum of the throw and maintain lingering contact (zanshin).

The word zanshin is a Japanese term that refers to maintaining a lingering focus or connection with your training partner after you have thrown them.

Let go and move away to the appropriate distance, just out of striking distance. Keep the soft eye focus, maintaining a lingering focus or concentration between yourself and your training partner after the completion of all techniques. Maintain an awareness of your environment, as if sensing, and being ready for, the next attack. Bow to show respect.

A Breath Throw against an Opposite-Hand Grab (Ai–hanmi Kokyu–nage), #1

First, bow to show respect. Then establish a centered, balanced, neutral ready stance at the appropriate distance, just out of striking range. Establish and maintain a soft eye focus through your training partner's eyes. Relax your breathing and your body. Calm your mind.

Your training partner approaches and grabs your wrist with his opposite hand (ai-hanmi). Immediately enter and blend by cross-stepping forward off the attack-line and twisting his arm upward (see Figure 12-12a). Inhale as you enter and blend. The pressure on his wrist will cause his elbow to lower as his

Figure 12-12a: Ai-hanmi kokyu-nage #1, first part   Figure 12-12b: Ai-hanmi kokyu-nage #1, second part

arm twists and begin the take his balance forward. Your training partner will try to correct his balance by pulling back. By this time, you have stepped behind your training partner and have lightly placed your hands on his shoulders (see Figure 12-12b). Step backward and off his fall line as you pull down toward his balance point, which is one shin's length behind his centerline, to

Figure 12-12c: Ai-hanmi kokyu-nage #1, third part

throw him. Exhale as you throw. Maintain your own posture (see Figure 12-12c).

Let go and move away to the appropriate distance, just out of striking distance. Keep the soft eye focus, maintaining a lingering focus or concentration between yourself and your training partner after the completion of all techniques. Maintain an awareness of your environment, as if sensing, and being ready for, the next attack. Bow to show respect.

A Breath Throw against an Opposite-Hand Grab (Ai-hanmi Kokyu-nage), #2

First, bow to show respect. Then establish a centered, balanced, neutral ready stance at the appropriate distance, just out of striking range. Establish and maintain a soft eye focus through your training partner's eyes. Relax your breathing and your body. Calm your mind.

Your training partner approaches and grabs your wrist with the opposite hand (ai-hanmi). Immediately inhale as you enter and blend with his attack by sliding forward slightly off the attack-line. Rotate your wrist so that your palm faces forward, and turn his hand over, thumb down. Allow his hand to continue forward without resistance on the same attack line and at the same level (see Figure 12-13a). Pull his hand forward to help him overextend, take his balance, and maintain momentum. Pivot from your center as he passes you, and apply forward pressure to the back of his elbow. Going down on one knee helps to empty the space for him, making him lose his

Practice throws with a sense of cooperation, not competition. Help your training partner to train and learn how to apply techniques effectively by:

☞ not resisting a throw with muscle strength, yet

☞ not just complying with being thrown.

Figure 12-13a: Ai-hanmi kokyu-nage #2,
first part

Figure 12-13b: Ai-hanmi kokyu-nage #2, second part

balance. This will allow you to add your body weight to the momentum and power of the throw. Exhale as you throw. Continue to follow through and throw your training partner on the same attack line he initiated (see Figure 12-13b).

Let go and move away to the appropriate distance, just out of striking distance. Keep the soft eye focus, maintaining a lingering focus or concentration between yourself and your training partner after the completion of all techniques. Maintain an awareness of your environment, as if sensing, and being ready for, the next attack. Bow to show respect.

Advanced Aikido Throws

There are several advanced throwing techniques. They include the hip throw (*koshi-nage*), the cross-arm throw (*juji-nage*), a leg pick up and drop throw, throws in which you drop and sacrifice your own balance, and throws that are based totally on timing and never touch your training partner. The approach and attack of your training partner can be from your back (*ushiro*), when kneeling (suwari-waza), or with your training partner standing while you are kneeling (*hanmi-handachi*).

There are infinite possibilities to the combination of aikido throws, as well as counters to each throw.

chapter 13

locking and
pinning techniques

THERE ARE FIVE PRIMARY aikido pinning, or joint-control, techniques. These techniques work by setting up and moving the muscular and skeletal system of your opponent into specific angles that he or she is unable to break out of. The techniques are: (1)the arm lock (*ikkyo*), (2) the wrist turn-in lock (*nikyo*), (3) the wrist-twist lock (*sankyo*), (4) the inside wrist lock (*yonkyo*), and (5) the wrist lock (*gokyo*).

Immobilization techniques (*katame-waza*) are based on arm-lock techniques. When practicing these techniques, remember that it is possible to extend the lock into a pin by taking your training partner face down onto the mat. Maintain control by adjusting your stance and the distance between yourself and your training partner.

> There are five primary aikido pinning, or joint-control, techniques. These locking techniques follow the numbering system: the first is *ikkyo*, the arm lock; the second is *nikyo*, the wrist turn-in lock; the third is *sankyo*, the wrist-twist lock; the fourth is *yonkyo*, the inside wrist lock; and the fifth is *gokyo*, the wrist lock.

Tapping Out

Your and your training partner must learn to signal, or tap out, to let the one applying the lock (tori) know when enough pressure has been applied to the wrist joint lock. The tori must learn to go slowly and smoothly. Any jerking motion can dislocate or harm the training partner's wrist. The tori must pay close attention to placement of the hands and to pressure. In joint locks, the difference of a fraction of an inch, a degree of angle, sometimes a slight turn or twist, makes a great difference in effectiveness. The uke must learn to tap out to indicate that the tori has applied enough pressure to produce

Tapping out is accomplished by tapping or slapping the mat or your training partner twice to signal submission. Waiting too long to tap out will only result in your own injury. Pay attention to your training partner's tap-outs so that you don't injure them.

pain and submission. These techniques can lock, control, or immobilize your training partner.

The Arm Lock (Ikkyo)

Ikkyo is often the first arm pin technique one learns for securing or controlling through wrist-joint locks. Many other techniques are based on ikkyo ude-osae, so it is important to start your training with it. Ikkyo was first designed to break the elbow joint. It is used now as a means to throw as well as pin your training partner. This lock creates pain by pinning the elbow joint to the mat in a fully extended position, while compressing the ulnar nerve.

First, bow to show respect, then establish a centered, balanced, neutral ready stance at the appropriate distance, just out of striking range. Establish and maintain a soft eye focus through your training partner's eyes. Relax your breathing and your body. Calm your mind.

Figure 13-1a: Ikkyo, first part

As your partner steps in and grabs you in a same-hand (gyaku-hanmi) grip, blend by slightly stepping back with his oncoming momentum. Swing both hands up in hand blades, one to his face and the other to his wrist. Slide the ridge of your hand down his arm to his wrist as you pull him forward and down to break his balance. In an upward circular motion, redirect by turning his wrist over, bending his elbow, and pushing his elbow in the direction of his ear, taking his balance and turning his body as you step forward (see Figure 13-1a). Continue your circular motion until your partner is face down on the mat and controlled. Extend his arm so his wrist is higher than his shoulder,

Figure 13-1b: Ikkyo, second part

and apply pressure on his elbow and wrist until your training partner taps out in submission (see Figure 13-1b).

Let go and move away to the appropriate distance, just out of striking distance. Keep the soft eye focus, maintaining a lingering focus or concentration between yourself and your training partner after the completion of all techniques. Maintain an awareness of your environment, as if sensing, and being ready for, the next attack. Bow to show respect.

Arm-Lock Variations *(Henka-waza Ikkyo)*
Arm Lock Applied to the Front against a Same-Hand Grab *(Ai-hanmi Ikkyo Omote)*

As your training partner comes forward, use your hand blade to the wrist as soon as he grabs your wrist. Swing your arm up in a circular spiral motion. Maintaining control of his arm with your hand blade, break his balance. Step forward and pin him face down, with his right arm extended, keeping your hand blade on his elbow.

Arm Lock Applied to the Rear against a Same-Hand Grab *(Ai-hanmi Ikkyo Ura)*

As the training partner comes forward, slide your left foot forward toward your training partner's right side. Pivot and take control of his right arm until he is on the ground. Keep your hand on his elbow.

Arm Lock Applied to the Front against an Overhead Strike *(Shomen-uchi Ikkyo Omote)*

When your training partner attempts to strike at your face, stop with both hand blades. Step forward and through, holding the wrist and elbow. Pin him from the kneeling (seiza) position.

Arm Lock Applied to the Rear against an Overhead Strike
(*Shomen-uchi Ikkyo Ura*)

When your training partner attempts to strike you with an overhead attack, take his arm by the wrist and elbow with both your hand blades, and then grab. Take a wide pivot and take him down. Turn and pin him from a kneeling (seiza) position.

Arm Lock Applied to the Front against a Diagonal Head or Neck Strike
(*Yokomen-uchi Ikkyo Omote*)

When your training partner attempts to strike you with a diagonal right hand blade, step in to the front. Pivot as you take control of his wrist with your right hand blade and grab. Break his balance by stepping in and swinging his hand up in a circular spiral motion. Then bring his arm down and pin him face down in a kneeling (seiza) position.

Arm Lock Applied to the Rear against a Diagonal Head or Neck Strike
(*Yokomen-uchi Ikkyo Ura*)

When your training partner tries to strike the side of your face with his hand blade, advance fast and thrust your own hand blade to his arm and face. Take his wrist and elbow with your hand blades and grab. Pivot behind him while you swing his arm up in a circular spiral motion and then down, taking his balance. Continue until he is pinned in a face down position.

Figure 13-2a: Nikyo

Wrist Turn-in Lock (Nikyo)

Nikyo is a joint lock that produces extreme pain when applied correctly, and controls your training partner by attacking his or her will to continue to fight. Nikyo bends and twists your training partner's wrist, causing immediate sharp pain and an automatic bending of the knees to ease the pressure. The common explanation for the pain is that the technique puts pressure

Figure 13-2b: Nikyo (close-up)

on the nerve, stretches the joint, and strains the tendon, muscle, and ligament. Forcing the smallest wrist bone against the large bone of the forearm results in the painful stimulation of the nerve in the bony surfaces.

Wrist Turn-in Lock Applied against a Same-Hand Grab (Ai-hanmi Nikyo)

First, bow to show respect. Then establish a centered, balanced, neutral ready stance at the appropriate distance, just out of striking range. Establish and maintain a soft eye focus through your training partner's eyes. Relax your breathing and your body. Calm your mind.

As your training partner approaches and grabs your wrist across your centerline, enter and blend with his approach by sliding back slightly and off his attack line. Rotate your wrist until it is on top of his wrist and his hand is pointed thumb down. His wrist and elbow should be bent at ninety degrees, forming an S-shape, with his arm parallel to the ground. Secure his hand with your free hand. Apply the wrist turn-in lock (nikyo) by slightly twisting the hand upward while pressing down on the elbow, as shown in Figure 13-2b. The pain will stop his momentum and encourage submission.

Let go and move away to the appropriate distance, just out of striking distance. Keep the soft eye focus, maintaining a lingering focus or concentration between yourself and your training partner after the completion of all techniques. Maintain an awareness of your environment, as if sensing, and being ready for, the next attack. Bow to show respect.

Wrist Turn-in Lock Applied to an Opposite-Hand Grab (Gyaku-hanmi Nikyo)

First, bow to show respect. Then establish a centered, balanced, neutral ready stance at the appropriate distance, just out of striking range. Establish and maintain a soft eye focus through your training partner's eyes. Relax your breathing and your body. Calm your mind.

As your training partner steps in and grabs you with his opposite hand (gyaku-hanmi), step to the outside (ura) to get off the line of attack. Rotate your wrist until it is on top of your training partner's hand, which is now thumb down. Secure his trapped hand with your free one. Notice the S-shaped curves of the arm with ninety-degree angles at the wrist and elbow. The arm is parallel to the ground. Lean in, bending his elbow and applying downward and inward pressure on his forearm to bring his elbow down, while maintaining the hand position.

Let go and move away to the appropriate distance, just out of striking distance. Keep the soft eye focus, maintaining a lingering focus or concentration between yourself and your training partner after the completion of all techniques. Maintain an awareness of your environment, as if sensing, and being ready for, the next attack. Bow to show respect.

Variations of the Wrist Turn-in Locking Technique (Henka-waza Nikyo)

Wrist Turn-in Lock Applied to the Front against an Opposite-Hand Grab (Gyaku-hanmi Nikyo Omote)

When your training partner grabs your left wrist with his right hand (gyaku-hanmi), step in and apply your hand blade or strike (atemi) to his face. Bring your hand blade down his arm to his wrist, pulling him to break his balance. Bring his arm up in an arc, and use your left hand blade on his right elbow to break his balance in the opposite direction. Apply the wrist turn-in lock (nikyo) by establishing the S-shape with his arm and pressing.

Wrist Turn-in Lock Applied to the Rear against an Opposite-Hand Grab (Gyaku-hanmi Nikyo Ura)

As your training partner grabs your right wrist with his left hand (gyaku-hanmi), enter forward and take your hand blades up into his face and then down his arm. Pull forward to break his balance. Control his right hand with your left hand by securing it into your shoulder socket. With your left hand, force his right elbow into the S-shape of nikyo. Push the elbow out and pivot (tenkan), putting him face down. Place your knees on opposite sides of his shoulder and apply an arm-lock pin.

Wrist Turn-in Lock Applied against a Double-Hand Grab (Ryote-dori Nikyo)

Your training partner approaches and grabs both of your wrists with both hands (ryote-dori). Enter and blend by sliding back slightly to overextend your training partner's arms and begin to break his or her balance. Rotate both of your wrists outward and over your training partner's wrists until they are upside down, with the thumbs pointing to the ground. Both arms form an S-shape with ninety-degree angles at the wrist and elbow, and are parallel to the ground. With the ridge blade of your hand, apply nikyo by pressing downward on both trapped wrists at once. As your training partner bends his or her knees to reduce the pain, you can push backward (ura) or pull forward (omote) to throw or control.

Wrist Turn-in Lock Applied to the Front against a Double-Hand Grab on One Wrist (Morote-dori Nikyo Omote)

Your training partner gasps your left forearm or wrist using both of his hands (morote-dori). Enter by stepping into him, and arch his arm upward. Control his elbow and turn him back into the direction he was coming from, breaking his balance. Use your body weight and hand blade to control him. Hold his left wrist with your left hand blade, and his left elbow with your right hand blade. Push forward (omote), breaking his balance, and pin him face down. Squeeze his shoulder between your knees and apply nikyo in the S-shaped lock.

Wrist Turn-in Lock Applied to the Rear against a Double-Hand Grab on One Wrist (Morote-dori Nikyo Ura)

Your training partner grabs your left wrist with both hands (morote-dori). Raise both of your hand blades. Using a spiral motion, pivot (tenkan) backward (ura). Use both of your hands on your training partner's wrist to trap and lock it. Arch his arm up again into an S-shaped nikyo lock by controlling and holding his hand into your shoulder socket with your right hand, and pushing down on the elbow with the right hand. The torque created by holding and twisting the hand and elbow in opposite directions produces great pain. Break his balance until he taps out. Arch his arm up again and pivot (tenkan) behind (ura) to pin him face down. Squeeze his shoulders between your knees as you kneel next to him and apply a submission arm lock.

Wrist-Twist Lock Technique (Sankyo Waza)

The sankyo lock can be applied as a standing technique or used as a take down, and is applied by twisting the wrist in a direction that it was not designed to go in. This twist is quite painful. An important point in executing this technique is to firmly grab the back of your training partner's hand and to twist it before pivoting to his front as you take control of his or her elbow. Notice that

Figure 13-3a: Sankyo

the sankyo lock is very different from the ikkyo and nikyo locks.

Wrist-Twist Lock Applied against a Same-Hand Grab (Ai-hanmi Sankyo)

First, bow to show respect. Then establish a centered, balanced, neutral ready stance at the appropriate distance, just out of striking range. Establish and maintain a soft eye focus through your training partner's eyes. Relax your breathing and your body. Calm your mind.

Your training partner approaches and grabs your hand with the same hand (ai-hanmi). Enter by stepping in off the attack line and pivoting (tenkan) until you are behind your training partner. As you move your body, circle over his hand until your hand is palm up and his hand is vertical. Pull and twist the hand by turning your body and lifting the elbow slightly until the arm forms a ninety-degree angle. Your training partner will rise onto his toes, breaking his balance (see Figure 13-3a). You can continue his momentum backward (ura), by bringing the wrist of the locked hand forward (omote) for a throw (nage), or you can bend the wrist palm down and toward the rear and pivot behind (ura) for a take down.

Figure 13-3b: Sankyo (close-up)

Let go and move away to the appropriate distance, just out of striking distance. Keep the soft eye focus, maintaining a lingering focus or concentration between yourself and your training partner after the completion of all techniques. Maintain an awareness of your environment, as if sensing, and being ready for, the next attack. Bow to show respect.

Variations of the Wrist-Twist Lock (*Henka-waza Sankyo*)

A common variation of the wrist-twist lock (sankyo), referred to as *mawashi*, is used when your training partner is already face down on the ground. It is a combination of sankyo and an arm-bar. Pin your training partner by using your hand to firmly grab and twist the back of his hand as you hold it to your shoulder. Lock his arm in place with your arm across his elbow. A slight lean will produce pain in his shoulder area. Apply pressure slowly and steadily—never

The word *mawashi* is the Japanese term that refers to the combination of sankyo and an arm bar. An arm bar is executed by holding the arm straight as a bar and applying pressure to the elbow, forcing it to lock out and producing a great deal of pain and potential damage.

jerk your movement. A quick motion can produce severe pain, injury, and damage. Enough pressure will encourage a submission signal (tapping twice). Release the pressure.

Wrist-Twist Lock Applied to the Front against an Opposite-Hand Grab (*Gyaku-hanmi Sankyo Omote*)

Your training partner approaches and grabs your wrist with his opposite hand (gyaku-hanmi). Enter by stepping in. Strike (atemi) to his face to distract him from his grab and to mentally begin to take his balance. Scrape your hand blade down the inside of his arm on the bone, and grab his wrist. This same action pulls and takes his balance. Twist and turn the arm, first upward and then down, in circular motions, to break his balance. Reach around and grab his wrist in a sankyo lock. Twist and pull his hand into your chest, allowing your training partner to rise slightly. Pivot (tenkan) in front of him and pull him forward (omote) into a face down pin. Apply mawashi until he taps out.

Wrist Twist Lock Applied to the Rear against an Opposite-Hand Grab (*Gyaku-hanmi Sankyo Ura*)

Your training partner approaches and grabs your wrist with his opposite hand (gyaku-hanmi). Enter by stepping in while simultaneously swinging your hand blade up to strike (atemi) at his face. Scrape your hand blade down the inside of his arm on the bone to the wrist and pull to break his balance. Push his elbow forward in upward circular motions to further break his balance and control him. Reach under his hand and grab it in a sankyo lock. Step behind (ura), pivot (tenkan), and pull him into a face down pin. Apply mawashi until he taps out.

Wrist-Twist Lock Applied to the Front against an Overhead Strike (*Shomen-uchi Sankyo Omote*)

As your training partner steps in, attempting to strike down at your face (shomen-uchi), enter by stepping forward. Simultaneously intercept his strike and control his arm with your double hand blades at his wrist and elbow. Continue the forward momentum, turning him until he is facing the same direction as you are. Keep pushing his arm in a circular path forward and down with your hand blades, breaking his balance. Grab his hand in a sankyo lock. Pull and step to the front, pulling until he is pinned face down. Apply mawashi until he taps out.

Wrist-Twist Lock Applied to the Rear against an Overhead Strike (*Shomen-uchi Sankyo Ura*)

As your training partner steps in and strikes down (shomen-uchi), step in and enter with a rising double hand blade, intercepting the strike (shomen-uchi) at his wrist and elbow. Your forward momentum turns your training partner's body so he is now facing the same direction that you are. Reach under and grab his hand in a sankyo lock, step to the rear (ura), and pivot (tenkan). Maintaining the sankyo lock, pull and pin him and apply mawashi until he taps out.

Wrist-Twist Lock Applied to the Front against a Diagonal Strike (*Yokomen-uchi Sankyo Omote*)

Your training partner attacks, attempting to strike your head or neck with a diagonal or oblique strike (yokomen-uchi). Step forward, enter, and blend by pivoting (tenkan) to his front. Swing your two hand blades up to intercept and control his attacking arm. One of your hand blades goes to his wrist to control the arm. The other strikes (atemi) to his face before repositioning to his elbow. Break his balance by controlling his hand and elbow. Pull forward toward his balance point in order to break his balance. Reach under and grab his wrist in a sankyo lock. Locking his arm, pivot step (tenkan) to the front and pull his arm to put him in a face down pin. Apply mawashi until he taps out.

Wrist-Twist Lock Applied to the Rear against a Diagonal Strike (*Yokomen-uchi Sankyo Ura*)

Your training partner attacks, attempting a diagonal oblique strike (yokomen-uchi) to your face. Swiftly step in while his striking hand is still back, before it breaks his own body line. Intercept his attacking arm with your double hand blade to control his arm, and strike (atemi) to his face. Slide your striking hand down and under his elbow, raising and controlling it. Step under his arm and cross-step behind him. Apply downward pressure to rotate his elbow forward, bending him over and breaking his balance. Grab his wrist in a sankyo lock. Pull and twist his hand to control the elbow and continue breaking his balance. Pivot step (tenkan) behind him (ura) and pull him into a face down pin. Apply mawashi until he taps out.

Inside Wrist Lock (Yonkyo)

Yonkyo, the fourth type of wrist securing, is designed to attack a weak point on your training partner's inside wrist, the pulse point. Precise application of yonkyo on a point on the forearm just a few inches up from the thumb, on the inside of the wrist bone, produces great pain. Yonkyo can be applied standing, or as an aid to a take down. An important point in executing this technique as a take down is to firmly grab the back of your training partner's wrist and to twist it before pivoting to his or her front as you take control of the elbow.

Inside Wrist Lock against an Opposite-Hand Grab (*Gyaku-hanmi Yonkyo*)

First, bow to show respect. Then establish a centered, balanced, neutral ready stance at the appropriate distance, just out of striking range. Establish and maintain a soft eye focus through your training partner's eyes. Relax your breathing and your body. Calm your mind.

Your training partner approaches and grabs you with his opposite hand (gyaku-hanmi). You enter and blend by stepping in off the attack line, intercepting the attacking hand before it can make contact and interrupting your training partner's momentum and balance. As he grabs your wrist, rotate your hand over so your hand is palm down and his hand is palm up (see Figure 13-4a). Hold his hand in place, bending his wrist upward while pressing on the yonkyo pressure point with the inside of the knuckle of your index finger. To give your index finger the required force, hold it extended, rather than using

Figure 13-4a: Yonkyo

it to grasp his wrist (see Figure 13-4b). Apply pressure and control him until he taps out.

Let go and move away to the appropriate distance, just out of striking distance. Keep your soft eye focus, maintaining a lingering focus or concentration between yourself and your training partner after the completion of all techniques. Maintain an awareness of your environment, as if sensing, and being ready for, the next attack. Bow to show respect.

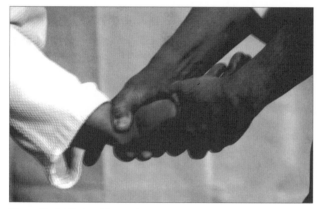

Figure 13-4b: Yonkyo (close-up)

Variations of the Inside Wrist Lock *(Henka-waza Yonkyo)*
Inside Wrist Lock Applied to the Front against a Same-Hand Grab *(Ai-hanmi Yonkyo Omote)*

As your training partner steps in and grabs your hand with the same hand (ai-hanmi), pull back and simultaneously make a small circular hand and wrist rotation, to place your palm facing down on the top inside of your training partner's wrist. Extend your index finger to expose your first knuckle bone, and push it against the yonkyo nerve point on the wrist.

Inside Wrist Lock Applied to the Front against an Opposite-Hand Grab
(Gyaku-hanmi Omote Yonkyo)

As your training partner grabs your wrist with the opposite hand (gyaku-hanmi), enter by stepping in and swinging up both your hand blades. One of your hand blades strikes to the face. Your other hand blade intercepts and controls your training partner's arm. Slide your striking hand down to his elbow and wrist. Rotate his arm over to break his balance, and pull him into a face down pin. Slide your hand into yonkyo position, and apply pressure until he taps out.

Inside Wrist Lock Applied to the Front against a Double-Hand Grab
(*Ryote-dori Yonkyo Omote*)

Your training partner steps forward and grabs both your wrists with his two hands (ryote-dori). Enter by stepping in and swinging both of your hand blades up. One of your hand blades strikes at (atemi) the face, while the other intercepts and control his arm. After you strike or feint (atemi) to his face, slide your hands down his arm to the wrist. Reach over his hand and grab his wrist. Twisting his wrist and pulling it toward your chest will pick him up slightly. Rotate his arm up and over in a circular motion, controlling both his wrist and elbow. Continue the rotation to break his balance and pull him forward. Reach over his hand and grab his wrist, putting pressure on the pulse point and twisting (yonkyo). Continue your forward momentum (omote) until he is face down. Keep your hands in the yonkyo position. Apply pressure until he taps out.

Inside Wrist Lock Applied to the Rear against a Double-Hand Grab
(*Ryote-dori Yonkyo Ura*)

Your training partner advances forward and grabs both your wrists with both his hands (ryote-dori). Enter by stepping forward and swinging both your hand blades up. After a strike (atemi) or feint to his face, bring your hands down, scraping his arm to the wrist. Pull his arm slightly to take his balance. Grab his wrist and turn it over. Cross-step and pivot (tenkan) behind (ura) him. Reach over his hand and grab his wrist. Twisting the wrist while bringing his hand back into your chest will pick him up slightly. Switch hands to apply pressure to the pulse point (yonkyo). Hold his wrist with both of your hands. Continue to pivot (tenkan) to his back (ura) until he is in a face down pin. Maintain your hold on his wrist in a yonkyo position. Apply pressure until he taps out.

Inside Wrist Lock Applied to the Front against a Diagonal Strike (*Yokomen-uchi Yonkyo Omote*)

Your training partner advances and attempts a diagonal strike (yokomen-uchi) to the side of your neck or head. Enter by stepping forward and swinging both your hands up in a double hand blade to intercept and control your training partner's striking arm. One of your hand blades strikes or feints (atemi) to the face. Pivot step (tenkan) toward his back, blending and allowing the path of his strike to continue forward (omote). An overextension of the strike will break his balance. Reverse the direction by rotating his elbow upward while applying pressure to the pulse point (yonkyo)—again, breaking his balance or keeping him unbalanced. Continue the rotation into a face down pin. Maintain your hold on the wrist and apply yonkyo. Apply pressure until your training partner taps out.

Inside Wrist Lock Applied to the Rear against a Diagonal Strike (*Yokomen-uchi Yonkyo Ura*)

Your training partner approaches and attempts a diagonal (yokomen-uchi) strike to your head or neck. Swiftly enter by advancing and swinging up both your hands in a double hand blade to intercept and control his striking arm before it crosses his body line coming forward. One of your hand blades strikes or feints (atemi) to his face, while the other stops the forward momentum of his striking arm. The strike (atemi) or feint to his face begins to break his balance by causing him to lean or flinch backward to avoid being hit. Slide your hand under his elbow and rotate it forward to break his balance. Slide your hands to the wrist. Step and pivot (tenkan) behind (ura) him while pulling him into a face down pin. Apply pressure to the yonkyo point until your training partner taps out.

Ground Wrist Pin Technique (Gokyo)

The fifth pinning technique, gokyo, was originally designed and used as a ground pin and a disarming technique for knife (*tanto*) attacks. To perform gokyo, unlike ikkyo, it is important to grasp your training partner's wrist from underneath and firmly pull it down. Gokyo works by manipulating the tissue on the back of the wrist, close to the second hand-bone (which terminates in the index finger). The pain of this pinning technique is due to the manipulation of the wrist joint and the wrist-to-hand ligaments. This technique forces the arm into an S-shaped bend similar to the one seen in the nikkyo pin, but the hand is pinned against the ground in gokyo, not against the body, as in nikyo.

Ground Wrist Pin (Gokyo)

First, bow to show respect. Then establish a centered, balanced, neutral ready stance at the appropriate distance, just out of striking range. Establish and maintain a soft eye focus through your training partner's eyes. Relax your breathing and your body. Calm your mind.

Figure 13-5: Gokyo

As your training partner approaches and attacks, use any technique that leaves him in a face down position. Remember to enter and blend with his attack. Redirect and unbalance him. Maintain contact with him when throwing, to facilitate a controlled face down take down. Once he is face down, slide his hand, palm up, across the mat toward his face, until his hand is directly below his elbow (see Figure 13-5). Gradually apply pressure downward and slightly out to his elbow, to use the gokyo pin. Keep increasing the pressure until your training partner taps out.

Let go and move away to the appropriate distance, just out of striking distance. Keep the soft eye focus, maintaining a lingering focus or concentration between yourself and your training partner after the completion of all techniques. Maintain an awareness of your environment, as if sensing, and being ready for, the next attack. Bow to show respect.

Ground Wrist Pin Variations (Henka-waza Gokyo)
Ground Wrist Pin Applied to the Front against an Overhead Strike (Shomen-uchi Gokyo Omote)

Your training partner attempts a downward strike (shomen-uchi) to your head. Enter by swiftly stepping in and swinging both your hands up in two hand blades, to intercept his strike. Control his striking arm at the wrist with one of your hand blades. With your other hand blade, strike or feint (atemi) to his face, to interrupt his momentum and begin to break his balance. Slide your hand blades down his arm to control him at the elbow and wrist. Apply pressure at the pulse point on his wrist (yonkyo). Rotate his elbow over, and pivot (tenkan) in order to pull him into a face down pin. Slide his wrist toward his face until his elbow is directly over his wrist with a ninety-degree S-shaped bend at his elbow and wrist. Gradually apply downward pressure on his elbow and into the wrist until your training partner taps out.

Ground Wrist Pin Applied to the Rear against a Diagonal Strike (*Yokomen-uchi Gokyo Ura*)

From a standing ready position, your training partner attempts a diagonal strike (yokomen-uchi) to your head or neck. Enter by swiftly stepping in. Intercept the arm before it crosses his own body line by swinging up both your hands in hand blades. One of your hand blades strikes or feints (atemi) to his face, which begins to disrupt his balance. Your other hand blade intercepts and controls his striking arm. Slide the striking (atemi) hand blade down his arm and under his elbow. Rotate his elbow as you pivot step (tenkan) behind (ura), breaking his balance and driving him into a face down pin. Slide his hand, palm up, with the back of his wrist toward his face, until his elbow is directly above his wrist in an S-shape. Gradually apply downward pressure directly on his elbow and into his wrist until your training partner taps out.

These three control pins, or joint locks, used to secure and control the wrist to unbalance and take down your training partner, are the key to advancing your aikido technique.

Advanced variations, combinations, and counter-techniques are infinite. It is beyond the scope of this basic book to present the topic in full and do it justice. All techniques can be countered or combined. These unlimited variations give aikido its fluidity and constantly changing and growing repertory. It can be said that aikido is a complete art in itself, but that it certainly is not finished.

There are infinite combinations of arm locks, especially when combined with throwing techniques.

part 4
applying the basics

AIKIDO PLACES a great emphasis on technical skill and ki development. The technical expertise provides an unobstructed flow of ki, but such proficiency can only be developed over time, through consistent and persistent training. As the subtleties of the techniques become clearer to you, the development, application, and extension of ki become a greater part of your training. As the techniques flow, you will be ready to apply your basic techniques in multiple-person attack exercises (*randori*) and freestyle technique exercises (*jiyu-waza*).

chapter 14
ki development

ENTRAL TO AIKIDO is the concept and development of ki. Some argue that aikido exists as a purely martial art, apart from an esoteric philosophy that teaches a universal energy. Others accept ki, develop it, and extend it into their aikido techniques and their lives.

What Is Ki?

At the heart of aikido is the concept of ki. Ki is each person's core energy, or essence of life, waiting to be realized, actualized, and expressed. Aikido is a discipline for discovering, developing, and demonstrating the existence and power of ki, which has many philosophical, metaphysical, and practical interpretations.

Ki refers to a universal life force or energy which connects us all physically and spiritually.

The Taoist philosophy of the Chinese sage Lao-tzu (sixth century B.C.) saw ki, or chi in Chinese, as the essential principle of harmony and the natural creative expression of the opposite forces of yin and yang. Mencius, a Chinese philosopher of the turn of the fourth century B.C., expressed ki as the courage of moral correctness, virtue, and righteousness. Kuan-tzu (720–645 B.C.), the prime minister of the state of Qi during the Zhou dynasty and master of ancient insight into political strategy, simply saw it as the divine energy that exists in all things.

Metaphysically, ki is the force, or energy, required and responsible for all movement and growth, from the budding and eventual withering of plants to the birth and death of the individual. The existence of ki means life and health. The absence of ki causes illness and death.

Taken on a practical level, ki flows throughout the body on an established course called a "meridian." The continuous unblocked flow of ki promotes health. The blockage of ki flow is responsible for illness. When ki leaves the body, one dies. The Eastern medical practices of acupuncture and acupressure remove blockage in ki flow and restore and promote health and vitality. For many years, Western medicine and science have denied the existence of ki flow and the effectiveness of Eastern medicine. The technology developed by the West to test new ideas may not be sufficiently subtle to measure and test ki, or the two medical philosophies may have developed along incompatible theoretical lines.

Once the concept of ki is initially accepted, one can begin to develop and extend it through aikido training. O'Sensei Morihei Ueshiba was a strong believer in ki, yet his insights are often difficult for the aikido student to understand. It is like trying to explain the flow of water to someone who does not understand gravity. O'Sensei Morihei Ueshiba saw that all things in the universe have ki in common. Therefore, ki becomes the link for unity of the body, mind, and spirit, the unifying force between self and others, the harmony between the attacker and the defender, and the energy that ties us all together. Ki is the reason that we either all win together or all lose together. Cutting the self off creates difference, separation, and alienation. Connecting and harmonizing with ki allows one to feel a part of a greater identity. This greater identity is beyond the simple ego identity; it is universal and spiritual.

Aikido connects and unifies the universal ki flow through the approaching opponent into the defender's body and mind, and allows for a peaceful and loving redirection of the momentum of conflict toward a positive end. Ki is both the unity of the individual with the universe and the spontaneous expression of that energy through the breath and execution of aikido techniques.

Ki Exercises

Ki development can be likened to water flowing through a hose. The first thing you want to do is to straighten the hose and get the kinks out. After you have the hose straightened out, you can turn the water on, and it flows freely. Physical alignment and technical proficiency allow ki to circulate through the body meridians, just as the water can flow through the untangled hose. Health is the free flow of energy with no blockage—where there is blockage there is illness. Remove the blockage, and health will happen on its own.

Physical Alignment and Technical Proficiency

Physical alignment concerns your body, both alone and in relationship to your training partner's body. Your physical alignment projects your ki directly and powerfully, while maintaining your centerline and executing your technique. When you practice successful aikido techniques on your training partner, you mis-align his skeletal and muscular systems so that he cannot resist your force or maintain balance.

A physical aspect of ki development involves the physical alignment of the body and technical proficiency in execution of the aikido technique.

There are several elements to physical body alignment. Part 3, "Learning the Basics," addressed these points, including stances, strikes, grabs, throws, and pins. One of the most important points of physical alignment is maintaining your centerline and staying centered. The centerline is an imaginary line running from the top of the head, through the body, and directly between the feet. Think of the centerline as a vertical pole around which your body rotates. It balances and centers the left and the right, the front and the back. Use the centerline to make sure that your toes, knees, hips, shoulders, and eyes all point in the same direction. The horizontal center of the body is located just below the navel. Where the vertical and horizontal centers of the body intersect becomes the point where all your movement originates.

The idea is to maintain your own physical alignment while disrupting your training partner's. Many of the throws and pins work because you have positioned your training partner's skeletal and muscular system at angles that do not support each other. The balance point is approximately one shin's length out to the front or back from the centerline, or the same length around either foot. Overextending past this distance does not allow the body to maintain balance. When you disrupt the physical alignment and aim your technique at your training partner's balance point, the slightest effort will force him or her to fall.

The way to establish this technical expertise is consistent and persistent training. One of the self-monitoring criteria for technical skill is how much you actually feel the technique as you execute it. Surprisingly, a good rule to remember is that if you can feel the technique too much, then you are probably using your muscles to force execution, which is unnecessary. When properly executed, the technique takes very little, or no, physical muscle force. Technical ability relies on technique, not force. This is consistent and compatible with the aikido principle of entering and blending rather than meeting force with more force or resistance.

Tohei Sensei's Ki-Society

Tohei Sensei (born in 1920) broke away from the Aikikai aikido schools of O'Sensei Morihei Ueshiba to develop a system of mind and body unification that placed greater emphasis on ki development. Tohei Sensei (Tohei 1973, p. 2; 1976, p. 15; 1978 p. 27) developed four rules that greatly help in the realization and expression of ki. He taught students to stay completely relaxed, to move from their center, to keep their weight to the underside, and to extend their ki.

While executing a technique, stay completely relaxed. Most people do not realize how tense their muscles really are. The body begins to experience tension as normal if held tensely for a period of time. An exercise to help feel the difference and develop relaxation is to progressively tense and release different muscle groups of the body. Tense the arm by making a tight fist. Hold the tension. Now open your hand and feel the difference as the arm relaxes. Continue this exercise through the rest of the muscle groups of the body. Take that same relaxation and continue it while executing your aikido technique.

Tohei Sensei advocated that you move from your center. Keep your body centered both vertically and horizontally. Move from the hip area. With all movement initiated from the hips, the technique gains all the power and momentum of the entire body.

For strength, there must be a strong foundation. A foundation comes from underneath. If you allow gravity to take its natural effect, the weight of anything will go to its lowest level. The weight will be on the underside. Your center will be where the weight of your upper body comes to rest over your legs in the hip region. You will feel more strength when you lift your arms if you feel as if the weight is pushing upward from the underside, rather than being lifted from above. To feel the power of ki when moving, move as if you were pushed forward from behind and underneath.

Extend your ki. Much as a ball continues on its own path after it leaves the throwing hand, your ki extends beyond your physical action.

Breathing and Breath Power

The basis of aikido is ki, or the unification of mind and body. Practicing breath power training helps you to focus on your inner energy. In aikido, the techniques use ki as their essence and power. Only with proper breathing can there be proper execution of aikido techniques. The two types of breath power practices are kneeling and standing.

To practice kneeling, sit opposite your training partner. As your training partner grabs both of your wrists (ryote-dori), apply pressure with the outside of your hand in a hand blade to the inside of his wrists. Swing your arms up in a circular spiral motion. Concentrate on your hand blade and focus on sending your ki through your arms and out your fingertips. Swing up and then throw your training partner to one side. Breathe in as you bring your training partner into your center. Breathe out as you execute the kokyu-nage, or breath throw.

Keep one continuous motion to maintain ki flow. Move as if you are keeping your connection with your training partner taut at all times.

To practice standing to the front, let your training partner grab your forearm with both of his hands (morote-dori). Step to the open side into an ai-hanmi position, form hand blades, and swing your arms up high and then down on your training partner in a kokyu-nage, or breath throw. To practice standing to the back, from gyaku-hanmi position, simply step in, making a wide pivot using a hand blade. Break your training partner's balance as you swing your arms up. Simultaneously breathe in as you extend your ki forward. Step back, and swing your hand down along with your training partner's arms with the hand blade to a kokyu-nage as you exhale.

Connection, Taking and Becoming the Center

The interchange between your training partner's center and your center becomes the basis for taking and becoming the center of the action. Think of yourself as a dot in the middle of a circle. Think of your training partner as another dot in the center of another circle. As your training partner approaches and attacks, the circles begin to merge and become more of an ellipse with two centers. As the merging continues, the centers and the circles become one. Take the center and become the center of the movement. This is the main process for entering and blending with the center.

Take and become the center with one fluid motion. Energy or ki flows in a continuous current without pause, unless it is blocked. To ensure the continual flow of ki in your technique, keep a steady rhythm. Initially you will learn your aikido technique step-by-step. Later, with consistent and persistent practice, you will begin to execute the entire technique in one fluid motion.

> When training, visualize your ki flowing through your training partner's center and slightly ahead of the direction of your technique.

Mental Projection

Mental projection can help you develop your ki. Ki directs the body, and the mind directs the ki flow. Several exercises illustrate the ability of your mind to unify with the ki flow in your body.

Applied kinesiology is the practice of muscle testing. Hold your arm out in front of you and have someone push down on your arm as you resist. Hold a positive thought or image in your mind, and have him or her test your muscle strength again. Now, hold a negative thought or image, and test. You will experience a definite loss of energy in your body with the negative thought or image. This suggests an explanation for the fact that fatigue often accompanies depression and negativity. Fear is one of the most common means to lose strength and interrupt your ki flow.

Another exercise is to place your hands on someone's shoulder. Keep your eyes on your hands and slowly walk forward while your training partner resists. Next, keeping your body relaxed, use a soft focus of the eyes at a distance through your partner, and again walk forward. Your training partner will have a harder time resisting your forward momentum.

The unbendable arm is another ki test that uses mental projection. Hold your arm out and have your training partner try to bend it. Next, imagine a metal bar attached to the wall behind you, extending through and underneath your entire arm, and anchored into the wall in front of you. Testing again will usually produce an unbendable arm. Another mental exercise is to imagine your arm as a continuous flow of water.

Take a centered, balanced, and natural stance. Have your training partner try to pick you up. Next, mentally project your center sinking beneath the ground. Anchor it there. Feel the solid foundation and relax your entire body. Your training partner will not be able to pick you up.

Do any of the muscle tests described here. Begin testing as you inhale and hold the mental image of the energy coming inwards to your center. Next, test during an exhalation as you hold the mental image of the energy projecting outward from your center.

Zanshin: Lingering Spirit

Zanshin is the lingering spirit of keeping your focus or concentration connected to your training partner after the execution of a technique. Keep your centered physical alignment and execute your technique with technical proficiency. Keep your body relaxed with the weight on the underside, project your ki, and hold it for a second or two after you have thrown your training partner.

Ki is mysterious, and many question its existence. It is the power generated from your center, about one inch below your navel, and it is developed over time with practice. Keeping the body relaxed and the hands open allows the ki to flow.

When first learning aikido techniques, you do not have to pay attention to changes in your training partner's ki. At that stage, the techniques are prearranged and practiced uniformly. As you gain proficiency, however, you will begin to sense the momentum, or ki, of your attacker. It is this sense that dictates the flow of the technique. Your training partner may sense a loss of continuity, momentum, or ki from you and step into a countermove. Ki requires the development of flexibility and the ability to change directions without losing any momentum.

It is this sense, the ability to enter and blend with the attacker's energy/ki that forms the foundation and philosophy of aikido.

chapter 15
randori and
jiyu-waza

AIKIDO BEGINNERS often feel frustrated by the lack of confrontation and contest in training. They tend to overlook the underlying philosophy of aikido that teaches a way to defend yourself without adding more damage to a situation. Persistent physical practice is the way to develop this mentality.

The techniques of aikido are physical demonstrations of its principles. It is through persistent training that a student will achieve the ability to stay relaxed and calm. This mental attitude, practiced inside the aikido school, benefits the student's life outside the school walls.

Inside the school, multiple-person attacks (randori) and freestyle exercises (jiyu-waza) are important ways to gain confidence in your training and in the power of aikido as a martial art. They are often much closer to reality than sparring for points with restrictive rules. Outside the school, demonstrations are the means to share your skills, honor your teacher (Sensei) and your school, and educate the public about the beauty and power of aikido.

Preparation and Participation
Rhythm and Pace: Slow and Relaxed
Don't forget to breathe. You can start by having one training partner stand in front of you and have another one stand behind you. Immediately after you finish the technique against the first training partner, turn and practice with the other. Alternate back and forth. As you take turns with your training partners, blend with both.

Timing is important in all aikido technique execution, but it is crucial in randori. It should be slow at first. Have your training partners walk toward you, rather than charge, on their approach and attack.

The timing, rhythm, and pace of randori should initially be very slow and relaxed, focusing on proper execution of the aikido technique and developing the ability to flow from one attacker to the next. Later the pace increases while you maintain a relaxed and confident attitude.

Limits

Limit the approach or attack and the defense technique. Later, as your training partners take their fall, have them approach and attack from where they land, instead of trying to stay in or return to strict practice lines. This changing of locations helps you to orient to them and not to your surrounding.

Soft Eye Focus (Me-tsuki)

Keep a soft eye focus. A soft focus keeps your peripheral vision sharp. Keep as many attackers in visual contact as possible. Try not to let anyone get behind you. Keep your head up. As soon as you engage one attacker, deal with him physically through your sense of touch, and then look around for the next one.

When practicing randori, don't stay in one place. Move around and keep moving. As you progress, you will find that you don't want to just stand there and wait for your training partners.

Maintain Your Center

As more training partners circle you, enter and blend, become and control the center of the technique, take their center and balance, throw, and move on. The flow of one technique enters and blends with the flow of the next technique. You become one continuous motion.

Control

Control your training partner's approach by your movement. By stepping backward, you can move off the line so that the angle of approach, by two different attackers, intersects. You can step out of the middle/center of two attackers coming at you from opposite sides, causing them to run into each other instead of you. You can hold on to one attacker and position him as a shield against another. You can throw one attacker in the direction of the next attacker and interrupt his forward momentum. Move so your attackers are all in a line, then simply deal with them one at a time.

Keep It Simple

Do not use fancy techniques that take too long, or try to pin an attacker during randori. You will leave yourself exposed to another attack. Enter forward and blend circularly. Do not back up or run away. Practice against a wall or in a corner to prevent too much backward movement. Simply deflect some attacks or move off the line and out of the way. If your technique isn't working, try something else.

Feints and Strikes (Atemi)

Use feints or strikes and yells to unbalance an attacker. Many people focus on the physical techniques during randori. Sometimes the best thing to do is deflect their attention and disrupt their balance through atemi and kiai.

Regularity

Practice randori regularly. Randori will improve your technique and your confidence.

The repetitive practice of any skill is what ensures mastery.

Free Style (Jiyu-waza)

Later, as you gain skill and confidence, change randori to jiyu-waza. Instead of limiting the approach or attack and the technique, allow your training partners to initiate any approach or attack they want. You also will begin to respond with any technique that feels appropriate. Start slowly and stay relaxed. At first, you will think of all the techniques you know and try to review them. As you progress, the approach or attack of your training partners will tell you the most appropriate response.

Practicing randori and jiyu-waza is one of the great joys of aikido. It gives you confidence in your training and yourself. It proves to you that aikido is a very powerful and effective martial art. Share the training harmoniously and peacefully with your training partner.

part 5
the training session

THE MOST IMPORTANT PART of aikido is the direct application of its principles. Aikido is more of a journey than a destination. Many people train to obtain their black belt. Others train for self-defense. Still others train for emotional expression, mental discipline, or even spiritual transformation. After a while, most train just to train. The training has become their identity. It is no longer what they do—the training becomes who they are.

You have chosen your school (*dojo*) and have shown up for classes. You are ready to apply the principles and basics of aikido. An old expression says that we do not rise to the level of our expectations, we fall to the level of our training. Train well.

chapter 16
warming up

WARMING UP is very important in any physical exercise program, because it prevents injuries and helps promote circulation and physical relaxation. In aikido, many of the warmup exercises (*junbi-taiso*) mimic the movements of the actual techniques you will do. The warmup exercises also provide a preparatory step for training with others. Do not neglect to warm up. The consequences may be that you won't be able to work out at all.

The warmup exercises in aikido include rotation of the upper body, bending and stretching the upper body forward and backward, bending and stretching the upper body to both sides, stretching of the legs and Achilles tendons,

 Warmup exercises prepare the body for training and incorporate most of the principles of aikido. They are an important part of every training session. Do not skip them.

rotation of the knees, exercises for the ankles and toes, exercises for the neck and shoulders, exercises for the wrist, and shaking to loosen the joints and gently massage the body.

Body and Ki Warmup Exercises

What follows is a sequence of exercises that are common to warming up in most aikido schools. Being familiar with these exercises will help you feel more comfortable at the beginning of class. When the instructor or sensei or one of his senior students leads the class through these exercises, follow him or her to the best of your ability. That ability will improve with practice. You can also use these warmup exercises for solo training. These exercises will aid you in your workout and in learning the techniques of aikido. Take them seriously and practice them regularly. Their effect is accumulative, meaning that the benefit will build up over time, even if you don't feel the immediate results.

Body Tapping

With fists, or open hands, tap the body all over. The purpose is to stimulate the circulatory system and get the blood flowing. Tap lightly on the arms from the wrist to the shoulders. Continue across the shoulders and chest and down the front of the body. Tap the insides and outsides of the legs, and back up to the lower back. Two variations are to use the fingertips or the palms. Continue until you feel a slight tingling throughout your body.

Neck Bends, Front and Back

Bend your head forward, touching your chin to your chest. Slowly and smoothly stretch your head backward as far as you can, to get a good stretch at the front and back of the neck. Inhale as you let your head go back. Exhale as you let your head come forward. Place your hands on your hips or in front on your center. Keep your back straight. Repeat 8 to 10 times.

Neck Bends, Side to Side

Bend your head slowly and smoothly to the left, stretching as far as possible. Repeat this stretch to the right, stretching the sides of the neck. Inhale as you move your head, and exhale as you let your head rest to one side. Keep your back straight with your hands on your hips or in front on your center. Repeat 8 to 10 times.

Neck Circles

Allow your head to drop forward, then rotate it slowly and smoothly in circles. Rotate the head in one direction and then the other, loosening the neck joints. Inhale as your head rises, and exhale as you lower it to the other side. Place your hands on your hips or in front on your waist, with your back straight as you do the rotations. Repeat 8 to 10 times.

Shoulder Rotations, Forward and Back

From the centerline of your body, slowly and smoothly swing your arms forward and down from the shoulders, several times. Slowly and smoothly swing your arms backward, loosening the shoulder joints. Inhale as the arms rise, and exhale as they lower. Keep your back straight. Maintain a soft eye focus forward. Repeat 8 to 10 times.

Side Bends

Raising your hands directly over your head, smoothly and slowly bend to one side as far as possible. Then bend to the other side, stretching the sides of the body. Inhale as you raise your body, and exhale as you bend into the side stretches. Keep a solid grounded stance. Maintain a soft eye focus forward. Repeat 8 to 10 times.

Body Bends, Front and Back

With feet wide apart, bend forward at the waist. With your hands, reach backward between your legs, as far as possible. Next, rise straight up from your centerline and stretch backward as far as possible. Inhale as your body transitions, and exhale as you hold the stretch. Keep your stance grounded and solid. Maintain a soft eye focus forward. Repeat 8 to 10 times.

Body Circles

With both hands held slightly above your head, bend forward at the waist as far as possible, until your hands touch the ground. Following a circular path to one side, continue until you are upright, bending backward as far as possible. Continue the circular path to the starting position. The circular path will be at a slight angle. Inhale as your body rises, and exhale as you come forward and down. Keep a solid and grounded stance. Maintain a soft eye focus forward. Repeat 8 to 10 times.

Long Leg Stretch

Start with a balanced, centered, natural stance. Slowly and smoothly lower yourself by bending one knee, keeping your heels on the ground. Stretch the other leg out sideways, pointing the toes toward the ceiling. Inhale as your body transitions, and exhale as you let your body lower into a long leg stretch. A variation is to either keep both feet flat on the floor or to rotate the stretched foot inward with the toes pointed upward, keeping the other heel flat on the floor. Try to keep your body balanced and centered over your legs as you move. Do not bend forward too much in an attempt to maintain balance. Maintain a soft eye focus forward. Repeat 8 to 10 times.

Hip Circles

With your hands on your hips, place your feet together, and rotate your hips in a horizontal circular motion, first to one side and then to the other. Keep your body straight with your head aligned over your feet, moving only the hips. Inhale as your hips move backward, and exhale as they come forward. Keep your back straight and your head level. Maintain a soft eye focus forward. Repeat 8 to 10 times.

Knee Bends and Toe Touches

Make sure your feet, knees, and hips are all aligned. Keeping your feet flat on the ground, slowly and smoothly squat, bending your knees at a ninety-degree angle, until your thighs are parallel to the ground. Do not bounce. Next, rise into an upright position. Then lean forward, keeping your back straight, and touch your toes. Exhale as you squat or bend to touch your toes, and inhale as you return to a standing position. Keep your back somewhat straight and your heels flat on the floor. Maintain a soft eye focus forward. Repeat 8 to 10 times.

Knee Circles

Place both hands on your knees. Keeping your upper body aligned over your feet, smoothly and slowly rotate your knees to one direction and then in the other. Inhale as your knees rotate to the side and back, and exhale as they come forward. Keep your head level and your heels flat on the floor. Maintain a soft eye focus forward (me-tsuki). Repeat 8 to 10 times.

> In aikido, push-ups are done on the wrists, unlike other martial arts that do them on the knuckles. Doing push-ups on the wrists develops their strength, flexibility, and tolerance for pain. This is important because so many aikido techniques work with the skeletal connectedness of the wrist.

Wrist Push-Ups

Assume a normal push-up position with your back straight. Turn your wrists over so the backs of your hands are on the mat. Instead of lowering your body vertically, dip your body forward in an arch as far as you can, with your head up and your hips down close to the mat. Inhale as your body comes upward, and exhale as you dip and go forward. Maintain a soft eye focus forward. Repeat 8 to 10 times.

Ankle Rotations and Foot Massage

From a sitting position, with legs stretched out in front of you, bring one foot to rest on top of the opposite thigh. Rotate your ankle forward and backward. Repeat 8 to 10 times in each direction. Loosen up and massage your toes by pulling and twisting them. Rub the bottom of your foot with your thumb, knuckles, or palm. The energy meridians in the body end at the soles of the feet. A good massage will not only improve your circulation and give you a sense of grounding in your feet, but will also stimulate your energy meridian and aid in your health. Slap both the top and bottom of your foot. Shake your foot. Repeat on the other foot. Maintain a soft eye focus forward.

Leg Stretches Forward, Left, and Right

Sit on the ground, spreading your legs as far apart as possible. Keeping your back straight, smoothly and slowly lean forward as far as possible, leading with your chest. Do not bounce. Next, alternate stretching directly over your left leg, then your right. Keep your back relatively straight and supple. Inhale as your body rises, and exhale as you lower into the stretch. Keep your knees down, with your toes pointed upward. Maintain a soft eye focus forward. Repeat 8 to 10 times.

Back Twists

From a seated position, keep your legs wide apart. Twist back toward your right, then your left. Attempt to place your hands directly behind you on your centerline to get a good stretch. Inhale as you come forward, and exhale as you stretch backward. It is all right to turn the legs and hips over slightly to aid in the stretch. Maintain a soft eye focus forward. Repeat 8 to 10 times.

Feet Together and Pull Down

Sitting upright, place the soles of your feet together. Holding your feet with your hands, slowly and smoothly bend forward. Keep your back straight, and attempt to bring your chest down to your feet. Inhale as you move into an upright position, and exhale as you bend forward. Maintain a soft eye focus forward. Repeat 8 to 10 times.

Knee Butterflies

Sit upright with the soles of your feet together. With a smooth and rhythmic motion, move your knees up and down in a butterfly-like motion. Attempt to push your knees down toward the mat. Keep your back straight and head level. Breathe deeply. Maintain a soft eye focus forward. Repeat 8 to 10 times.

The rollbacks in the warmup exercises will prepare you for the ukemi (falling and rolling) you will be practicing during aikido training.

Seated Rollbacks

Sitting upright with your feet straight out in front of you, roll backward. Allow your back to curve and your legs to follow naturally. Raising your head and looking at your belt keeps your head off the mat. Allow your hands to rest on the mat behind your head as you roll back. Exhale as you roll back. Inhale as you come forward to the start position. Maintain a soft eye focus forward. Repeat 8 to 10 times.

Seated Rollbacks and Slap

Sitting upright with your feet in front of you and your knees slightly bent, cross your hands in front of your chest. As you roll backward, allow your hands to slap the mat to absorb the motion. Exhale at the same time that your hands slap the mat. Inhale as you return to the start position. Maintain a soft eye focus forward. Repeat 8 to 10 times.

Prone Side-to-Side Roll and Slap

Assume the side break-fall position, with your lower leg stretched out behind you and your knee slightly bent. Your top leg is positioned with the sole of your foot flat on the mat and your knee bent and pointed upward. Stretch out your lower arm with a slight bend to slap the mat. Hold your top hand loosely over your waist. Alternate rolling from side to side, exhaling as you slap the mat. Maintain a soft eye focus forward. Repeat 8 to 10 times.

One-Knee Backward Roll

Start in a one-knee kneeling position. Bend your left leg at a ninety-degree angle, as if you were starting to stand up. Hold your right arm out to the side. Put your left hand over your shoulder, palm up. Stay relaxed and exhale as you sit down over your back leg, keeping your body rounded, and roll backward.

When doing wrist exercises, apply pressure smoothly and gradually. Do not make sudden or abrupt movements. You will recognize many of these exercises as conditioning for the receiving of various wrist locks.

Keep the momentum going, and bring the back leg forward. Maintain a soft eye focus forward. Repeat 8 to 10 times.

Wrist Turn-Out Exercise (Kote-gaeshi-undo)

With your right hand, hold your left wrist with your fingers pointed up. Stand straight. Hold your left hand, your fingers pointing up, on your centerline, at your chest level. Place your left hand on your belt with your palm up. Now, simply bend your wrist upward. Place your right palm across the back of your left hand and raise it to chest level. Exhaling, slowly and smoothly, lower your hands to your waist, stretching your wrist. Inhale as you bring your hand upward. Exhale as you lower and stretch it. Repeat 8 to 10 times for each side. Keep your back straight and your stance grounded. Most grips in aikido are with the thumb and last three fingers, leaving the index finger free. Keep your eyes softly focused forward on the distance.

Between each wrist stretching exercise, shake your wrist vigorously.

First Wrist Exercise (Ikkyo-undo)

Hold your wrist with your fingers pointed downwards along your centerline. Keep your fingers pointing downward and raise them from your waist to your chest. Exhale as you raise your hand, and inhale as you lower it. Keep your back straight and your stance grounded. Keep your eyes softly focused forward on the distance. Repeat 8 to 10 times for each hand.

Wrist Turn-in Exercise (Nikyo-undo)

Hold your wrist with your fingers pointing forward. Stretch your right arm directly forward on your centerline, with the ridge of your hand pointing upward. Place the palm of your left hand directly on the back of your right hand. Pull back both hands into your body, directly in front, and on your centerline. Exhale as you pull in, and inhale as your hands go forward. Keep your back straight and your stance grounded. Keep your eyes softly focused forward on the distance. Repeat 8 to 10 times for each hand.

Wrist Twist Exercise (*Sankyu-undo*)

Place your left hand at waist level, palm down, on your centerline. Reach underneath your left hand with your right palm up, crossing your palms. Grip the fingers of your left hand. Slowly and smoothly raise your left hand up to your left side until your bicep is horizontal and your forearm is perpendicular to the ground, with the palm of your left hand facing outward. Exhale as you move your arm outward, and inhale as you bring your arm back in. Keep your back straight and your stance grounded. Keep your eyes softly focused forward on the distance. Repeat 8 to 10 times for each hand.

Fingers Forward and Down

Place your left hand, palm up, on your centerline at your chest, close to your body. Place your right palm on the fingers of your left hand. In a circular motion, stretch your left arm forward then downwards, leading with your fingers. Try to lock out and extend your elbow until your palm is parallel to the floor and your arm is straight. Pulling up on your fingers in this position will add to the stretch. Exhale as your arm goes forward and out, and inhale as you bring it back in. Keep your back straight and your stance grounded. Keep your eyes softly focused forward on the distance. Repeat 8 to 10 times for each hand.

Rowing Exercise (*Funekogi-undo*)

Stand with your left foot in front of your body, in a relaxed stance, with your back straight and your body centered and balanced. Start with your arms held relaxed at your sides, then bring them straight forward to waist level as you push your body forward from your center and shout a loud kiai of "He." Relax, pull back with your hips along the same line, and shout "Ho." Allow your arms to return to your sides. Exhale as you move forward, and inhale as you come back. Emphasize both pushing out and pulling back equally. Keep your back straight and keep your stance grounded. Keep your eyes softly focused forward on the distance. Repeat 8 to 10 times with one foot forward in ai-hanmi, and then repeat with the other foot forward in gyaku-hanmi.

Blocking and Breath-Changing Exercise
(Shomen-uchi-ikkyo-undo or Kokyu Tenkan-ho)

Stand relaxed, centered, and balanced, with your arms naturally at your sides. Swing your arms upward to head level, as if to block a downward strike (shomen-uchi). Exhale as you push forward from your hips. Allow your arms to follow a natural curve, with your elbow slightly bent. Keep some tension in your arms throughout the movement. End as if you were pushing on the wall in front of you. Bring your arms back down, following the same natural curve to your sides, as you stand relaxed, centered, and balanced in the start position. Emphasize the pushing up and out equally with the pulling down and in. Keep your back straight and your stance grounded. Keep your eyes softly focused forward on the distance. Repeat 8 to 10 times with one foot forward in ai-hanmi, and then repeat with the other foot forward in gyaku-hanmi.

Body- and Breath-Turning Exercise
(Kokyu-ho or Tai-no-tenkan-ho)

Stand with your left foot in front of your body, in a relaxed stance, with your back straight and your body centered and balanced. Allow your hands to come forward on your centerline, at waist level, with your left hand leading. Stepping forward, and slightly off your centerline, reach forward with your right hand, palm-down. Scoop under with your hand and allow it to follow your centerline as you pivot (tenkan) your left foot 180 degrees. You are now facing the opposite direction. Think of your centerline as a flow of water that you dip your hand into, and allow it to follow the stream. Your body does not turn until your hand reaches your hips, and then your entire body turns as one. Keep your arms slightly extended, and end as if you were pushing on the opposite wall. Keep your back straight and your stance grounded. Keep your eyes softly focused forward on the distance. Repeat 8 to 10 times.

Hands-Up Breath-Turning Exercise (Shayu-undo)

With feet parallel, stand relaxed, balanced, and centered. Allow your arms to hang down naturally. Swing both hands up to your left on a natural arc, and twist at your waist in the same direction. As your hands reach the top of the arch, they will be slightly in front of your body-line. Exhale as you shift your weight to your left and twist at your waist. Allow your hands to swing down and to the opposite side. Keep your back straight and your stance grounded.

Keep your eyes softly focused forward on the distance. Repeat 8 to 10 times on each side.

Loosen the Shoulders

Stand in a relaxed, natural, balanced, and centered stance. Twist at your waist, swinging your arms from side to side. Your movement should begin from your center or hips. Keep your back straight and your stance grounded. Keep your eyes softly focused forward on the distance. Repeat 8 to 10 times.

 The solo practice of tenkan, the circular pivoting step unique to aikido, will increase the effectiveness of your technique by adding full-body coordination and power to each move.

Footwork Exercise, Ninety Degrees (*Tenkan Ashi-sabaki*)

Place your left foot forward in a relaxed, balanced, and centered stance. Step forward with your right foot slightly off your centerline. Next, move your body as one unit as you step in a ninety-degree turn. Your left foot will now be behind you. Keep your head and body at the same level as you turn. Do not bounce. Let your arms follow the movement initiated by your center or hips. Inhale as you move forward, and exhale as you move back into your stance. Keep your back straight and your stance grounded. Keep your eyes softly focused forward on the distance. Repeat 8 to 10 times.

Footwork Exercise, 180 Degrees (*Tenkan Ashi-sabaki*)

Place your right foot forward in a natural, balanced, and centered stance. Take a natural step forward. Swing your back foot around until you have turned 180 degrees and are facing the original direction. Inhale as you move forward, and exhale as you move backward into your stance. Keep your back straight and your stance grounded. Keep your eyes softly focused forward on the distance. Repeat 8 to 10 times.

Breathing Exercise

From a natural, balanced, and centered stance, allow your hands to slowly and smoothly rise as you inhale. Allow your hands to fall as you exhale. Pay attention, and exhale even more. Keep your back straight and your stance grounded. Keep your eyes softly focused forward on the distance. Repeat 8 to 10 times.

Forward Roll (Right/Left/Alternate)

Place your right foot forward. Lean forward and push off with your back leg. Smoothly and slowly roll up your right arm (held with some spring tension), across your right shoulder, diagonally to your left hip, and into a one-knee position. Exhale as you roll. The forward roll is easier if you hold the image of a circle in your mind. Let your upper body roll, and your legs will follow naturally. Keep your eyes softly focused forward on the distance. After doing continuous rolls on your right side, practice them on your left. Next, practice by alternating rolling right, taking a step, rolling left, taking a step, and rolling right again. Repeat 8 to 10 times.

Forward Roll to Backward Roll

After rolling forward, scoop your forward hand in one continuous motion backward over your head to lead your body momentum directly into a back roll. Inhale during the transitions, and exhale during the execution of the rolls. Keep your eyes softly focused forward on the distance. Repeat 8 to 10 times, forward right to backward left and forward left to backward right.

Break-Falls

Execute a forward roll allowing your body to extend and perform a break-fall. Land on one side with your bottom leg slightly extended, your top leg hitting on the sole of your foot, your bottom arm slapping the mat, and your top hand across your body, all hitting at the same time. Always exhale as you land on the mat. Keep your eyes softly focused forward on the distance. Repeat 8 to 10 times.

Obstacle Jumping

Rolls and break-falls (ukemi) can be practiced over obstacles such as another student's body. You can use any object as an obstacle. At first have the obstacle close to the ground and practice jumping and rolling over it. Do not focus on the obstacle, since your energy, or ki, will stop where your focus stops. Keep your eyes softly focused forward on the distance. You can increase the difficulty by adding another student to make it a longer horizontal jump and roll. You can also add to the height. Repeat 8 to 10 times.

Knee-Walking (Shikko)

Knee-walking, shikko, teaches correct body alignment and focuses on movement from your center or hips.

From a kneeling position, keeping your heels close together, lower yourself onto your forward knee. Pivot on your knee from your hip, bringing your back leg forward with your knee up. Keep your eyes softly focused forward on the distance. Shikko is an excellent way to increase your ability to move from your center or hips. You should eventually be able to perform all your techniques from a kneeling position (suwari-waza). Repeat 8 to 10 times.

Partner Warmups (*Sotaidosa-undo*)

Sotaidosa are partner exercises used, prior to training, as warmup exercises (junbi-taiso). There are several common variations.

Turning Stretch (*Tenkan-ho*)

As your training partner grabs your wrist, enter (irimi) and pivot (tenkan). Apply pressure with the outside blade of your hand to his wrist in a hand blade and pivot (tenkan) behind him, lifting his arms slightly. Inhale as you enter and blend, and exhale as you settle into the stretch. Keep your eyes softly focused forward on the distance. Repeat 8 to 10 times.

Entering Stretch (*Irimi*)

As your training partner grabs your wrist, enter by quickly moving forward, disrupting her balance with an irimi throw. Hold your position, at the furthest position possible from your training partner. Inhale as you move forward, and exhale with your execution of the stretch. Keep your eyes softly focused forward on the distance. Repeat 8 to 10 times.

Four-Direction Stretching (*Shiho-giri*)

As your training partner grabs your wrist, enter and blend, applying pressure with the outside edge of your hand in a hand blade, swinging your arms up.

Turn (tenkan) and swing your arms down. Stop just before throwing your training partner. Hold the stretch. Inhale as you enter and blend, exhale as you hold the stretch. Keep your eyes softly focused forward on the distance (me-tsuki). Repeat 8 to 10 times.

Double Arm Stretch, Front (*Ryote-dori Omote*)

As your training partner grabs both your wrists in a ryote-dori grip, apply pressure with the outside of your wrists to the inside of both of her wrists. Take an entering step forward (irimi omote), pivot (tenkan), then bring your hands down and hold the stretch. Move to the front and the back. Inhale as you move forward, and slowly exhale as you then settle into the stretch. Keep your eyes softly focused forward on the distance. Repeat 8 to 10 times.

Double Arm Stretch Rear (*Ryote-dori Ura*)

Your training partner grabs both your wrists in a ryote-dori grip. You imme-diately apply pressure with the outside of your hands in a hand blade to the inside of both wrists. Pivot widely and to your training partner's back (ura). Pull your hands down to stretch and hold. Inhale as you enter and blend, and exhale as you execute, then settle into the stretch. Keep your eyes softly focused forward on the distance. Repeat 8 to 10 times.

Warmups and cool downs are an important part of every training session. Do not start or end without them.

You will find that the warmup exercises described in this chapter will become an essential part of your aikido training. Practiced on a daily basis, warmup exercises will help you progress safely. In addition, these exercises are a great way to cool down after training.

Pay close attention to correct form, even in the warmup exercises. Do no movement sloppily. Your form matters, and your breathing matters. Keep your body aligned, balanced, and centered, and keep your eyes softly focused directly out in front of you at all times. Keep your eyes and mind concen-trated on what you are doing, and do not let them wander. The warmup exer-cises become a meditation in their own right. Paying attention to details helps you make correct form and attitude part of your aikido training.

chapter 17
how to participate
in a workout

O'SENSEI MORIHEI UESHIBA stressed that the student should always practice aikido in a vibrant and joyful manner. He designed aikido to be a spiritual, as well as a martial, practice. He felt that the world needed to learn to live in peace and harmony. The place to start was in the training hall. He said that instructors only impart a fraction of the teaching, and that it is only through your own practice that the mysteries of aikido come to life.

There are three people involved in your training workout. The first is your instructor. If you selected him well, he will be competent in his technique as well as his teaching. Many feel that, to progress in aikido, one must eventually teach. Teaching beginners forces you to always keep the basics in mind. To be a good teacher, you must always remember how to be a good student. The second person is you. Following the school rules of participation will help you have a safe and productive workout. The third is your training partner. In many ways, learning to be a good training partner is one of the hardest lessons in aikido.

Basic Requirements for Participation

Each organization has its own requirements for participation and its own rules of conduct inside the school. Usually these are posted, and you will be required to follow them. Find them and read them thoroughly. If you don't understand them, ask. A clarification can save you a lot of embarrassment. Your attendance at a school will be taken as implied consent to follow these rules of conduct and participation. Know what you are agreeing to. Here are some guidelines to follow in your aikido training:

Observe Etiquette and Respect

The first rule of budo is that everything begins and ends with etiquette. Etiquette is respect. Bowing is one way that aikido shows this respect. Bow to your instructor. Bow to your training partner. Etiquette is sitting and standing straight, so don't wobble. Etiquette is silence.

Be Polite

Etiquette is also being polite. The best way to be polite is by being safe to train with. The no-horseplay rule is there for the safety of everyone. Be careful. Safety always comes first.

Be considerate to all fellow members. Arrive on time for class. Listen to your teacher. Follow instructions. Keep a positive attitude. Never wear street shoes on the mat. Bow before and after entering the mat, at its edge. If arriving late, bow and enter the mat, kneel and bow to O'Sensei, bow to your chief instructor, and bow to all black belts. Bow to each other before and after practice. Bow to any black belt offering you assistance and instruction.

Obey Your Instructor

Aikido is capable of killing an opponent with one blow. Obey the instructor, and do not make practice a time for needless testing of strength. You will never master aikido if you are unwilling to follow the instructor's teaching.

Always Be on Your Guard

Since aikido is a martial art, one person learns to face many opponents simultaneously. This requires that you polish and perfect the execution of each movement, so you can take on not only the training partner directly in front of you but also those approaching from other directions.

Enjoy the Practice of Aikido

Your study of aikido should be pleasant, so that you learn to maintain a positive attitude and a peaceful heart. A positive attitude gives you more strength to train with and motivation to continue training.

You Are Responsible for Your Training

Your instructor can only teach you a small fraction of what you will learn. Your mastery will depend almost entirely on your own practice. Do not be satisfied simply with what you get in class. While the class gives you much to digest and practice, there is so much more to learn. You must take responsibility for your own growth and progression and not rely on the instructor to do it for you. There are thousands of techniques and variations and combinations. Be more concerned with the quality of the techniques you learn than with the quantity. Repetition of the basics is the key to improvement and mastery.

> Aikido depends on technical proficiency, not force. Working up to your limits will help you to expand them. Working too much, too fast, and beyond them, will create injuries. Train intelligently and wisely.

Never Force Yourself beyond Your Natural Range

Be reasonable in your practice. Begin daily practice with light movements of the body, gradually increasing the intensity and strength of your movements. Never overexert yourself. Your whole posture can become unbalanced from overexertion, so moderation is the key. In this way, even the elderly can attain their goals in training with pleasure and without bodily harm.

Attend Classes Consistently

The need for consistent attendance and participation cannot be overstressed. Progress in any art depends on the discipline to show up consistently and to practice the techniques. At times, this may be difficult. If you attend morning class, you may not want to get out of bed. If you attend evening class, you may be tired after a long day at work and just want to have your supper and watch some TV. There are many reasons for not wanting to train, but there are no real excuses. You cannot progress if you do not show up.

There is a saying that the wise go for progress, not perfection. While many programs suggest that you should always give 110 to 200 percent, the emphasis on perfection may actually take away from your training. Therefore, it may be best for you to make only a 98-percent effort. The 2 percent margin for error may just give you the permission you need to try a new move or to take a fall.

Train Repetitively

When learning something new in aikido, you will probably need many training sessions to gain some sense of technical mastery. As illustrated throughout this book, ideas and principles are repeated frequently to allow you to begin to recognize and respond to them. Be patient as you practice. An old expression says that you never step into the same stream twice. Each time you practice a technique, it will be different. Each person you train with will provide you with a different energy.

Be Clean

Everyone appreciates good personal hygiene. Please bathe, shave if necessary, and brush your teeth before each practice session. Keep your uniform clean and in good repair. Cut and file fingernails and toenails to prevent injuries. Always help clean the mat and school after you work out.

Train Properly

Sit silently and watch when the head instructor is demonstrating. There is no excess talking or socializing during class. Help those students junior to you, and gratefully accept instruction from those senior to you. Take turns with your training partner. Be both the giver and the receiver. Taking turns is another way to practice blending and to learn your techniques from different perspectives.

Train consistently and persistently for progress, not perfection. Just relax, breathe, and enjoy yourself.

Discipline

Discipline is training in accordance to rules, a code of conduct, and a training ethic. Discipline is about showing up for yourself, for your training partners, and for your school.

Understand your purpose and the benefits of training. Enjoy yourself and have enthusiasm about training. Become absorbed in your training, focus on it. Discipline takes time to develop, but you can gain discipline by keeping your motivation spontaneous, by continual repetition, by planning goals and objectives, and by commitment to mastery and effectiveness. Discipline is showing up, dressing out, and working out to the best of your ability on that day, at that time. Over time, in all you do, you will see the benefits of the discipline you gain in training.

Being a Good Training Partner

When you first encounter aikido, you think of how to do the techniques. That is half of the art. The other half is learning to be a good training partner and to receive the techniques. This is the art of seeing beyond yourself and giving yourself to your partner. You are still training and will receive valuable insights into the principles and applications of the techniques by having them practiced upon you. You are there to train, but also to help others train.

To help them train, you must give just the right amount of commitment and resistance. In the beginning stages of training, it is easy to resist the application of the technique. The hard part is resisting the need to resist. This is not a power struggle. Your training partner is learning. Let him. Help him. At first, grab or strike slowly and easily. Follow him as he moves you. Don't be too helpful. Don't give him the technique. Make him work the principles and applications. Over time, with practice, you will be required and requested to increase your commitment and resistance until you will be approaching and attacking with full speed and force.

A part of learning to cooperate in training, instead of competing, comes from losing yourself and allowing your training partner to benefit from his training with you. We do not learn much about ourselves in isolation. It is in relationship with others that we make our greatest discoveries. Do you enter and blend creating harmony, or do you engage in competitive power struggles? Are you patient with others as they learn, or do you only want to be right and have your turn?

Learn to keep your balance and center, physically and mentally, while others find theirs through training with you.

Outside Your Dojo

Do not gossip or speak for other people, or about other people, at your school. Never make commitments for the school, unless asked and authorized to. Do not teach others aikido, unless asked and authorized to do so.

Never criticize or insult other styles of martial arts. Practice nonviolent conflict resolution at all times in all matters. Practice personal and social responsibility at all times in all matters. One of the best ways to explain aikido to others is to show them by your example, not tell them. Be a model of what aikido can offer.

We do not rise to the level of our expectations, we fall to the level of our training. How you train is how you will fight. Training is a reflection of your attitude toward your life. Train well because your life, and the lives of your loved ones, may depend on it.

chapter 18
mental training

THERE ARE FOUR DISTINCT STAGES in the acquisition of skills. The first two are physical: Physical training includes the learning of the general basic muscle skills and the precise technical muscle skills. They are necessary for proper execution of the techniques. The other two are mental: The mental stages include the tactical (intellectual) skills and the psychological (character traits) skills.

Training Body and Mind

Wherever the mind goes, the body tends to follow. The opposite is also true—wherever the body goes, the head tends to follow. Instead of remaining caught up in the either/or bind of having to choose between training the body or the mind, the wise student will train both. Mental training is the responsibility of the student, while the school focuses on physical participation.

Mental training is one of the most important parts of training in aikido, or any activity in life. It is amazing that it is also one of the most neglected areas of training. Many assume that if they train the body, the mind will just naturally get it. While there is some truth to that, it is very far from being the whole story.

The body will not do what it is not told to do. The mind must tell it what to do and how to do it, in order for it to respond accordingly.

Training in aikido can be painful. Most of that pain comes from mistakes and errors due to ignorance. These mistakes and errors call for correction, not judgment or punishment, and you can make corrections only when you apply the right attitude, perception, or knowledge to the situation—mental disciplines.

Mental training will never replace physical training. Don't just train physically harder, train more intelligently.

Mental Training

Education

The first step to mental training is education. Read everything you can get your hands on about aikido. The local school, college, and public libraries are great places to start and to gain a free education. It is surprising to find how many aikido books most public library systems have. It may also surprise you to find aikido books at stores that sell used books. Talk with the owners of these stores and tell them what you want, and they will search for it, or let you know when a copy comes in. Most local bookstores have a large sports section in which you will usually find a few aikido books. Do not forget the online sources for used books, discussion forums, mail lists, and bulletin boards.

> The mind cannot make decisions based on information it doesn't have. The better the information you have, the better the decisions you can make, and the better your training will be.

Overcoming Negative Thoughts (Fear, Anger, and Stress)

Fear, anger, and stress are three of the primary negative thought patterns that you can overcome by seeing through them to their origin, and understanding how you create them.

Fear is a fantasy. To overcome fear, understand its origin. No one is afraid of training, but many are afraid of their negative fantasy of what will happen if they do train. People are not afraid of falling or taking hard break-falls (ukemi), they are afraid that it will hurt too much. This fantasy can come true if you don't train consistently and persistently. No one is afraid of jumping over an obstacle, but of hurting someone and getting hurt. Students are not afraid of offering a committed attack, they are afraid that their training partner isn't ready. Without the internal fantasy, there is no fear. Let go of fantasies by staying externally focused and aware, and the fears will leave.

Anger has a pattern, too. Think of the last time that you got angry about something. You don't get in trouble for being angry, it is how you express your anger that causes problems. Learn nonviolent, constructive ways to deal with anger. Anger usually comes from the hurt feeling we have because we have taken something personally. Training in aikido helps one to learn not to take attacks personally and to respond in appropriate, nonviolent ways.

Stress is actually two thoughts that oppose each other. There will be times when a part of you doesn't want to train. Another part will push you to go. This internal tug-of-war creates stress. Stress is like doing a dynamic isometric exercise. Slowly push your hand forward while simultaneously holding it back. Let go of one of the thoughts, and the stress will disappear. Remind yourself how good you feel after a workout and how it will add to your consistent and persistent training so you can feel good about yourself.

Think of other feelings or emotions that may get in the way of your training. Become aware of the thoughts that create those feelings or emotions. Discovering how your negative thoughts create your negative feelings and emotions will allow you to begin to loosen their power over you. To unify the body and mind, you must send them both the same message, without resistance or objection.

While negative emotions and thoughts will physically weaken you, positive thoughts and emotions will strengthen you.

Maintaining a Positive Attitude

As you read in chapter 14, "Ki Development," positive thoughts add to your strength and ki flow, while negative thoughts take away your strength and block your ki flow. Maintaining a positive attitude will assist you during your training at the school and in your everyday life.

One way to transform negative thoughts into positive ones is to discover the positive intention behind the negative thoughts. In the case of anger, the positive intention is protection. Are there other, nonviolent ways of protecting yourself that are more effective and efficient? That is one reason many people study aikido. Beneath the anger is the hurt. Feelings are trying to tell us something. They may have simply been trying to get your attention. They may want you to take better care of yourself. Listen for their positive intention. When we take things seriously and personally, we feel more powerful and important, but many of the ways we react in those situations are not conducive to fulfilling those positive intentions. Find another way. Try to see the positive in all you do and in what others are doing.

Automate the Mental Process

Most martial arts focus on physical training of the body in techniques. There is a series of internal mental processes that can actually help speed up your reaction time. Do you ever wonder why some people are faster than others? Some of it may be that they have sped up their internal mental processing so that they don't have to go through the entire process every time a situation confronts them.

> With practice, you will find that your internal mental process can speed up and reduce your reaction time.

When your training partner approaches you and attempts an attack, you first need to perceive his movement. You build this awareness through both physical and mental practice. Once you become aware of the approach or attack, you need to assess what it is and the level of threat that it is to you. Not all approaches are attacks, and not all attacks require a full response. Some may just require you to get off the attack line. Each situation triggers the mental process of selecting the appropriate response for the given approach or attack. Once you have gone through all the possible responses, you need to select one. If you don't select one, you will become frozen. Having too many options can be like having no options at all. It can be overwhelming. Once you make a decision, your brain sends signals to the appropriate muscle groups for a response technique. Awareness of this internal processing of information is the first step to subjecting the process to direct mental training.

Mental Rehearsal

Mental rehearsal is an important part of mental training. Imagine yourself performing a technique. If the internal images are strong enough, the brain cells that control the muscles will respond in the same way—in the same order—as if you had actually performed the technique. If you mentally rehearse—or mentally practice—it repeatedly, eventually the cells will respond in the correct sequence automatically, and your performance of the technique will improve. The body responds better and faster to visual information. Telling yourself what to do is relatively slow. It takes much less time to get off the line than to say the words, "get off the line." There are several steps you can take to get the most of your mental rehearsal.

Mental Rehearsal to Acquire New Skills

Maintaining center is an important concept in aikido. Let's see how to rehearse mentally the establishing and maintaining of your center.

Take a deep breath. Allow your body to become relaxed, and let your mind be calm and open. Identify the concept or principle you want to incorporate into your training. In this case, we have selected maintaining your center. Next, state the principle as a personal belief: "I believe in maintaining my center before, during, and after a technique." Change that belief into a decision: "I will maintain my center before, during, and after a technique." Change that belief and decision into an experience: "I experience and feel my center before, during, and after a technique."

Create a mental movie from a spectator's or coach's point of view. Project the movie right in front of you by envisioning yourself maintaining your center before, during, and after a technique. Check to make sure that in your mental movie you are moving from the hip region, keeping your back straight.

Once you have the movie you want, step into it. This associated participator position allows your neurology to come into play. As you watch the movie from the inside, you may begin to feel your body starting to move, mimicking the technique. To enhance the experience, make sure the movie is in color, not black-and-white, large, clearly focused, and extending to your right (the usual mental position for the future). Run the movie several times, with the feeling that you have practiced the technique hundreds of times. Think of the next time you will want to establish and maintain your center. Make an association to an external cue that will trigger the centered feeling. Watch your movie from inside this future context and content. Find another future time, and run it repeatedly. Watch the skill of establishing and maintaining your center happen all by itself, without any conscious effort or thought. Now bring all that mental and neurological training back with you. Ask yourself if there is any part of you that objects to this new skill of establishing and maintaining your center. If there is, find the positive intention of that objection, and a way to use it to become even more centered.

Take this new skill of maintaining your center and create an internal movie of yourself accepting and maintaining your center as your new identity. It is not just what you do—allow it to become who you are. Notice how it affects your identity. See and feel how it enhances every aspect of your life. Extend the effects further, and see how they fit with your values and vision in life. Make a statement or affirmation that reconfirms this new skill and identity of maintaining your center. Relax your body. Take a deep breath. Congratulate yourself. This exercise encourages you to integrate a new skill with your identity, helping to habituate and automate the performance of the actual technique.

Mental Rehearsal to Unlearn Old Habits

Many use mental rehearsal to unlearn an unwanted skill, or to break out of a performance slump. In order to do this, select a behavior you no longer want. Many people, when they first come to aikido, have a tendency to back up, or chamber, all their movements before entering. Many people have a tendency to move their body backward, to back up, or to pull their arm or leg back, chambering before initiating forward movement. This can be the product of traditional training. Many use chambering in order to gain power, but it can slow your technique and reaction/response time.

Think of a time that you stepped backward or moved your arm backward before entering or moving forward. Experience this movement as a participant. You may be used to this position. This behavior has its positive benefits or intentions. Moving backward or chambering is also a means to establish distance for safety or to build power.

Now look at it as a spectator or a coach, from the outside. Notice how moving backward before entering actually moves your center away from the direction you want to go. You can make yourself even more vulnerable if you withdraw without getting off the line. The backward movement of your hands or hips is a great way to let your training partner know exactly what you are going to do, and give him or her time to anticipate and counter it. Moving backward or chambering actually telegraphs your movements.

Take your objective external spectator movie and make it into a black-and-white still. Push the still away from you and down to your left (the position usually associated with the past). How does it feel now?

Think of a person who just moved forward without chambering when entering. Watch that movie. Now step into it as described for mentally rehearsing the acquisition of a new skill.

Skill Anchors

Many use mental training to associate, or anchor, skills to a particular trigger. Let's say you want to learn to stay relaxed and calm as your training partner approaches or attacks you. You may have some history in which you had the experience of being hurt. You may have some fear response. Note the fear pattern mentioned earlier, and discover the internal negative fantasy you use to keep yourself from being relaxed and calm.

It is interesting to note that when we are relaxed and calm, our minds are not particularly busy. When we are tense and fearful, our minds are very busy. That is why it is important to look at how you stop yourself from being relaxed and calm.

Think of a time that you were relaxed and calm. Step into the experience and feel it. Say the words "relaxed and calm" to yourself. Turn up the intensity of the feeling each time you repeat, "relaxed and calm." Repeat and build up the association between the feelings and your resource anchor or trigger phrase, "relaxed and calm." Repeat until the mere thought of the words "relaxed and calm" make you actually feel relaxed and calm. Now step out of the past picture, but maintain the feeling and the association, or anchor, of saying, "relaxed and calm."

Create a movie of your training partner approaching to attack you. As he does, say the words, "relaxed and calm." Feel your body become relaxed and calm as it begins to associate these new feelings of relaxation and calmness with this new context of being approached and attacked. Repeat this several times until you naturally and automatically feel relaxed and calm as you picture your training partner approaching you to attack.

Next time you step onto the mat and actually have your training partner approaching you to attack, repeat the associated skill anchor. Feel your body respond with this new skill. Keep repeating several times until becoming relaxed and calm is natural and automatic.

Motivation

There are two main directions of motivation. You tend to either move "toward" or "away from" something. Understanding your motivational strategy can aid you in consistent and persistent training in aikido.

The "toward" strategy of motivation focuses on rewards and goals. A reward can be anything that you value. Some people need to have immediate rewards. Others may have more long-term goals that motivate them. This motivational

Many mental discipline practices are concentration exercises in that they work because you focus or concentrate on a specific behavior or sequence, such as mental rehearsal. Some meditation techniques are also concentration techniques. Other meditation techniques call for a letting go of all thoughts.

strategy pulls you toward what you want.

The "away" motivational strategy focuses on punishments and negative consequences. What will happen if you don't train consistently and persistently? This motivational strategy pushes you from behind to get away from, or avoid, something. It does not necessarily move you in the direction you want to go.

A combination of these two main directions produces a powerfully compelling strategy. Remember why you decided to train in aikido. Remind yourself of the immediate and long-term negative consequences of not training, and remind yourself of the immediate and long-term rewards and goals of your training.

Meditation

For a long time, many cultures and traditions have used meditation as a means of mental training. Many meditation techniques are actually concentration exercises that help focus and calm the mind. These schools of meditation have you focus on a specific visual picture or mandala. As your mind wanders, bring it back to where you want to keep your focus. Another school of meditation may give you a word or phrase to chant repeatedly to yourself or aloud. The internal chanting becomes the focus of your attention and awareness. Again, as the mind wanders, bring it back to the sound, phrase, or word you are trying to focus on.

The two types of meditation, or concentration, techniques mentioned give you some specific content to focus on. This single focus creates a sense of relaxation and calm by producing alpha brain waves.

Besides techniques that focus on specific "content," other meditation schools use a "process" technique. It is not what you meditate on, but the meditation process itself that becomes the technique. As thoughts come to mind, any thoughts, just acknowledge them and let them go. Do not look any deeper. Accept your thoughts and any external stimuli for what they are. Develop a detached observer state of mind. Allow yourself to stay externally focused on the flow of what is. This mental clarity, along with your consistent and persistent training in aikido, leads to the ability to detect any threat and respond appropriately.

Mushin

Mushin is the state of no-mind or empty-mind. It is a state where what you observe, and who you are, blend into one. The watcher and the watched become the same. It is a loss of personal ego identity and boundaries, and an acceptance of your oneness with the universe. This is the state of mind, or no-mind, that O'Sensei Morihei Ueshiba wants us all to aspire to for the spontaneous execution of technique.

chapter 19
self-defense

THIS BOOK has repeatedly stressed that the art of aikido is indeed a martial art. The techniques of aikido lend themselves very well to a self-defense situation. Though the self-defense techniques are somewhat harder to master, aikido is a powerful and effective tool for defending yourself—or others.

While self-defense is a major focus of most martial arts, it is never to be considered at a basic level or taken for granted.

Many of the ideas presented here for self-defense were developed in discussion with other martial artists dedicated to presenting and teaching realistic principles and techniques.

Aikido's Effectiveness in Self-Defense
The Basic Principles and Techniques
Many would say that if you have to use aikido in a self-defense situation, then you have not learned aikido. There is a tendency to believe that the study of aikido will help you to avoid the need to use it.

Contrary to what you might expect, it is usually the basic aikido principles and techniques that work best in a self-defense situation. Under stress, the body tends to lose the precise muscle coordination necessary to do advanced techniques. Self-defense is one of the most stressful situations you will ever find yourself in, so the basic, simple body movements of the aikido principles and techniques will be most useful to you. This is one of the reasons that aikido places such an emphasis on learning and relearning the fundamental principles and techniques. Only progressive, realistic repetition of the techniques gives you the skill to apply them in stressful, life-threatening, self-defense situations.

The practice of aikido principles has also been found useful for assessing and avoiding threatening situations. The best self-defense is never being in a position where you have to defend yourself.

The first stage of self-defense is an environmental awareness, which will help you avoid potentially dangerous situations.

Many martial artists question the effectiveness of aikido as a means of self-defense. Many people have not trained sufficiently to gain an effective mastery of the art. Others do not understand what aikido is. Size and strength do not matter in aikido. The relaxed body and calm mind, as developed by aikido, prepare you to defend yourself better than size and strength do. Aikido takes longer to master than other martial arts. Be patient and train persistently.

Environmental Awareness

Someone once said that one of the most important questions is whether we live in a safe world. Statistically, we do. Less than 10 percent of our population actually engages in any type of criminal activity. Less than 3 percent of the population is violent. Unfortunately, there are geographical pockets of people who make things appear much worse than they are. The wise person knows who and where these people are. This knowledge opens your training so you are able, and willing, to respond in an appropriate manner if you have the opportunity to save your own life or others'.

The first step in self-defense is to pay attention. Develop your environmental awareness. Most people walk through life without noticing what is going on around them. As you look around, are there things that seem out of place? Usually these are the environmental signs that something is wrong. People walking down the street all tend to walk at a similar pace. Is there anyone walking faster or slower? Identifying a potentially bad situation, and being able to avoid it, is an example of the aikido concept of getting off the line and avoiding the attack without ever making contact.

Environmental awareness can help you make the distinction between confrontations that are territorial and those that are predatory. A territorial dispute will happen because someone has gone past a boundary. The resolution of the confrontation is the reestablishment of the territorial boundary. There is usually a way to save face and make a safe exit. The goal of a predatory confrontation, on the other hand, is simply to get you. This is the dispute you really have to train for.

> Understand that attackers think differently than you do. Prepare yourself for an attack by understanding yourself and them.

Predators

Predators know their victims by their fear. In one study, researchers taped a video of a crowded street. They showed it to convicted muggers and robbers. The researchers asked them simply to say whom they would pick as their next target, or "mark." Consistently they all picked the same people. When researchers further analyzed those "marks," they noted that their body language—their gestures, posture, and movement—suggested a level of fear. By consistent and persist training in aikido, you will overcome the negative mental fantasies that create fear in the first place.

Many martial arts train you in preparation for attacks by a single individual. Unfortunately, predators often hunt in packs. By nature, predators have their own fear and live in a state of low self-esteem and poor communication skills. That is why they attack in the first place. The behavior of predators is fear-based in many ways, but understanding this does not excuse their behavior—it only explains it.

Most predatory attacks, especially when a weapon is involved, are ambushes and assassinations. Seldom will predators fight "fair." They will take every possible advantage, such as surprise and concealment. You may not see the attack coming, as you do in training at your school, so you must be prepared. Avoid the attack as best you can by keeping your distance and maintaining a soft eye focus, allowing you to detect your opponent's actions and respond to them much earlier.

Progression or Escalation

Predatory attacks do not just come out of nowhere. Most attacks follow a somewhat predictable pattern of progression and escalation (MacYoung, M., 1993). The four stages are: (1) potential and purpose, (2) probing, (3) positioning and posturing, and (4) pouncing. Being aware of this pattern can help you prepare to defend yourself and others, if needed.

Potential and purpose, the first stage of any attack, first builds up in the mind of the attacker. You see this in the attacker's eyes and posture. If some intuitive sense warns you to avoid a situation or person, trust that feeling. Most people are somewhat good at sensing danger. This is not paranoia, this is wisdom. Too often, we ask our rational mind to explain or justify these feelings. If they cannot be explained or justified, they are rejected, leaving us vulnerable to a pending attack and unprepared for it. Many people report that at one time they had some sense of pending danger that they unwisely ignored. Research supports that 93 percent of communication is nonverbal, so keep your eyes open. The predator is on a mission, looking for a target. Sometimes that target is very specific, but other times it is just convenient.

The next stage is the probe. The attacker will often make some type of probe in an attempt to identify you as an easy target. The probe may be as simple as looking at you to see if you will look away in fear or respond with a stare of competition. The probe may be a simple request for information, such as asking the time or asking for directions, or it may be as openly aggressive as swearing and name-calling. Anything to see how you will react. Clues of potential danger include an edge to a voice, sarcasm, mumbling, avoiding eye contact, blank stares, wringing of the hands, or any threatening gesture. The probe is both an opening "interview" and an attempt to bridge the gap or distance between you. Be aware and keep a safe distance and a soft eye focus.

After the probe, there is a stage of positioning or posturing. Often the attack is launched from this defensive stance. It can be a slight turning of the head, as if to look away from you, but more often they will start watching you from the corner of their eyes. It may be turning around a baseball cap, knocking the cap off his own head, or throwing his arms out to the side, exposing his chest and inviting an attack. This behavior is often like that of apes, who beat their chests and flail their arms in the air to scare off challengers. While this positioning or posturing gets your attention, it may also be a distraction, to let others attack. Remember predators often attack in packs. During the probe and the positioning, it is a good idea to keep your hands up and open, with the palms facing forward, establishing a fence. Keep a safe distance and keep circling until you can maneuver toward an escape route. Try not to escalate the problem or enter a power struggle by criticizing, insulting, ordering, threatening, ridiculing, arguing, raising your voice in tone or volume, or becoming too emotionally involved.

Verbal aikido skills can help you too. You may be able to enter and blend verbally, then redirect the conversation, giving you the opportunity to unbalance the attacker's intention and escape without fighting at all. An aikido response to the probe may be distracting, refocusing on the positives, changing the subject, or humor directed toward yourself, while taking their position seriously. Listening is an excellent way to deescalate potential danger. Let the person know you are listening by giving him your full attention, making eye contact without staring, nodding your head, saying "okay," and using other verbal means of repeating, reflecting, rephrasing, and reframing the situation. As in physical training, in which you avoid meeting an attack with your own force and resistance, you learn to enter, blend, and flow mentally and verbally with the attack. If the initial contact and probe begin to escalate, good manners and humor can sometimes redirect the mental attention of the attacker, so that he has no real reason to continue. During the positioning stage, the predator is looking for anything that can trigger and justify the pounce. Don't give him an excuse. Learn to be still physically, verbally, and mentally. This is not the stillness of a fear-based freeze response. This stillness comes from a quiet acceptance of what may be and a willingness to do whatever is necessary to survive.

The pounce or attack is actually fairly quick and brief. Unlike in the movies, real fights don't last very long. They only tend to last from thirty to ninety seconds. You are at a disadvantage, since your reaction to any attack is slower than the attack itself. Wise and realistic repetitive training in aikido will help you avoid attacks before they happen, or give you the tools and confidence to handle them. After the pounce or attack begins, there is an appropriate reaction or response. This is the application of the aikido techniques. Use only as much force as necessary—as little as possible. Aikido accepts that there are conflicts that will require your prompt physical intervention.

Aftermath
Physical Consequences
Attend to any injuries immediately. Get medical help.

Psychological Consequences
After an attack is over, there are several postattack effects. The trauma of being the victim of an attack may make you attempt to avoid anything that represents or symbolizes the original attack. There can be a high state of agi-

tation, hypervigilance, and paranoia. Thoughts, dreams, and nightmares may be so vivid that they actually trigger a re-experiencing of the trauma in flashbacks, as if it were happening all over again. Many need professional help to sort out their feelings and thoughts after being traumatized by an unexpected assault or attack. For some, it is as if the assault or attack does not belong on their personal internal map of the world. They have to find a way to make this most unpleasant event fit into their experience, in order to make some sense of the world they live in, now a different, unsafe world.

Legal Consequences

Another postattack effect is the intervention and investigation by law enforcement authorities. There are usually legal consequences to any use of violence. If the police are called, you will be asked to defend your actions. Always be respectful, polite, and honest when answering their questions. Please remember, very few people know the differences between martial arts. They will assume that if you practice a martial art, you have an advantage and your actions must be premeditated. You will need to show that you really believed you were facing real harm, and that you made every attempt possible to find an alternative to violence or the use of self-defense techniques.

Legally, an assault is any deliberate attempt to threaten or inflict injury upon another person. There has to be an apparent ability to inflict such injury. If you are the victim, you must believe that you should reasonably fear, or expect, immediate physical harm. This does not necessarily mean that your body is touched in any way. An "aggravated" assault is one that is intended to inflict injury—purposely, knowingly, recklessly, or through negligence and menace.

Investigation of an assault will include allegations and substantiation of all claims. All parties present will be questioned, including the victim, the offender, and any witnesses. The crime scene will be searched. The law enforcement authorities will want to know the motive, opportunity, and capability of the assailant. Background information may also be investigated to corroborate the stories given.

It is important that you demonstrate that you attempted to leave the scene, and that you attempted to stop the potential conflict verbally. In other words, you attempted, in front of a witness, to find a nonviolent resolution. You may also need to prove the necessity and appropriateness of the intent and intensity of your use of force in the situation. Many quick self-defense courses teach techniques that would not be considered an appropriate use of force.

The most important aspect of self-defense is developing a fighter's psychology, which will give you permission to follow through on what you have trained to do. The direct application of aikido in a self-defense situation is different than it is in the dojo, so you must train with this in mind.

These techniques would be considered overkill and very hard to justify.

A Fighter's Psychology

A fighter does not rely on a large arsenal of techniques. Fighters rely on knowing themselves and the principles of fighting.

To know yourself, you must be willing to make an honest inventory or search of what you are willing, and not willing, to do to protect yourself and others. If what you are trained to do, in the safety of your school, does not match who you are and what you are willing to do, it will not come into play in an actual fight. Hopefully, through training, you will begin to discover who you are. A fighter makes a commitment to do whatever is necessary.

An important distinction should be made between training, sparring, fighting, and combat. In training, you will rehearse drills to produce skills. The atmosphere is positive and nonthreatening. It is a learning environment where you gain experience. In sparring, you engage in competition, with set rules and boundaries. While it is a step up from training, and requires a different psychological mind-set, it is still a safe learning environment and experience. Real fighting is not safe, and it is not set up as a learning experience. You will, however, learn a lot about yourself from fighting. A fighter's psychology allows you to assess your own capabilities and the level of threat in the situation, and decide on the appropriate strategy. Combat implies that the threat assessment and appropriate response are fatal. The decision to enter combat means to accept the consequences of that decision, as well as the corresponding behavior.

Cross-Training

Whenever the discussion of self-defense comes up, the comparison of different martial arts styles appears. How does aikido handle a boxer's jab, cross, or hook? How does aikido handle kicks? How does aikido handle a wrestler or grappler? How does aikido handle a street fighter? How does aikido handle a knife or gun attack?

One of the best ways to know how to defend yourself against various attacks is to know that attack. The best defense against a boxer's jab, cross, or hook is to know how to execute them and what their weaknesses are. Many times, you can bob-and-weave until the opening appears where you can enter, blend, and disrupt your opponent's balance. Knowing how to kick allows you to better judge the distance. Grapplers and wrestlers can best be handled as they approach, before they attack. Keep your distance and pivot out of their grasp. When they go to the ground, try to be the one on top and in control. Street fighters combine fighting arts with sheer anger and can best be handled by avoiding them by any means. If you see them coming, get off their line of attack. When you understand the angles of attack and lines of projection for weapons, you have a better understanding of what you are up against and how best to defend yourself. Remember that nothing is worth your life.

Many do not advise cross-training in other martial arts too soon. There is wisdom to the idea of getting a good foundation in one art before you confuse yourself with another. Different people, with different abilities and capabilities, in different situations and environments, create arts for different reasons. They all have something to offer you. They all have strengths and weaknesses. Once you have a strong foundation in aikido, you may consider taking up another art to supplement or complement your current level of training. For self-defense purposes, you may want to study a striking, kicking, or grappling art to balance your training in aikido.

Technique

There are three main concepts in self-defense: clear, control, and counter. To clear an attack is to get off the attack line of the attacker's momentum. To control an attack, you enter and blend with it and begin to redirect and unbalance your attacker. To counter the attack, you can apply a throw or a locking and pinning technique. When necessary, strike the attacker.

The actual application of aikido techniques, in a self-defense situation, is far beyond the scope of this book and deserves volumes of its own. Suffice it to say here that the application of aikido techniques for self-defense would be different from the applications usually used in the typical school. Your techniques would be much quicker and crisper. The adrenaline rush and pump of a real conflict often limit precise muscle skills. Only those techniques that use more basic muscle skills will work.

If your interest is self-defense, train up slowly to a more realistic speed. Train with people who will give you a powerful and committed approach and attack. Many of the fancier techniques that primarily teach principles may not be appropriate or applicable in the streets. Many students periodically train to sharpen their self-defense skills. Train how you intend to fight.

Learn the three main concepts of self-defense: to clear, control, and counter.

Remember that training is not sparring. Sparring is not fighting. Fighting is not combat. Each has its own rules of engagement and appropriate use of force.

Aikido is excellent for self-defense. The best self-defense is to be aware of potential dangers, recognize them, and avoid them before they escalate into violence. It may take longer to learn how to be effective and efficient in the application of aikido to self-defense situations, but the techniques of aikido are sound and proven. Consistent and persistent training will give you the mental and physical awareness and confidence to avoid, or handle, most situations.

It is not the style of a martial art that makes it effective for self-defense. It is the willingness and training of the individual that make the technique effective.

part 6
making progress

THE BEST WAY to achieve success is to enjoy the process of training in aikido. To progress means that you are learning new techniques and practicing old ones. Progress comes from making a realistic assessment of where you are, setting a realistic goal, and having a realistic plan to get there. You have to know what you want, understand what you have to do to get it, and then do it. Aikido provides a means to make progress physically, mentally, and spiritually.

chapter 20

setting a goal
and setting up
a training program

O' SENSEI MORIHEI UESHIBA believed in three types of training. The first type harmonizes one's mind with the universe. The second harmonizes the body with the universe. The third harmonizes the ki.

As a new student, you may have some difficulty understanding and accepting the training program of aikido. It may appear that there is no real curriculum being followed. It may appear that people are just training to train. There is some truth to these observations. While there is always a curriculum being followed, they represent only a small portion of aikido, and the rest will unfold naturally during training. Be patient. Relax, breathe, and enjoy yourself. If you set a realistic long-term training goal, with a realistic short-term training objective, and consistently and persistently train with a realistic, but high, training ethic, you will reach your goal. You may even find that you enjoy your training so much that you train just to train. Sometimes losing sight of the goal, once set, is the best way to ensure that you achieve or surpass it. The goal and the process for achieving it become one.

Setting a Goal

Setting goals for your aikido training is not difficult. Research says that if you write your goals and objectives down and review them on a regular basis, there is a better likelihood that you will achieve them. Top athletes in all sports tend to keep an ongoing training log or journal. They set long-term goals and short-term objectives, and keep track of them on a daily basis. This is a great way to keep track of your progress. For many people, keeping track in a training log or journal is also a means to keep motivated. It provides a means to see your progress.

Your Long-Term Goal

There are several considerations in setting a goal. The goal needs to be stated in positive terms, be initiated and maintained by yourself, have clear criteria for success, both qualitative and quantitative, be attainable, be defined in terms of when and where the goal is to be demonstrated and obtained, and identify obstacles and resources.

What do you want? A goal is never stated in the negative. To set a goal of "don't choke" means to bring up all the mental mechanisms of choking. The mind will hold that image and send the message to the body to do exactly what you tell it not to do. A goal stated positively tells your body what you want from it, not what you don't want.

How will you know when you have achieved your goal? Goal setting gets very specific in its criteria for evidence. To state a goal clearly, you must know what you will see, hear, and feel. This will let you know, internally and externally, that you have obtained what you have sought and trained for. If your goal is simply to get your black belt (*shodan*), then you will know you have achieved it when your teacher presents you with your belt and certificate. But the study of aikido is both a lifelong goal and a lifelong process.

Is it within your control to achieve your goal? It should be. Many people set goals that are not within their power to reach. When they don't obtain their goal, they feel disappointed and defeated. It may not be up to you if you pass your test and receive your black belt. That is your teacher's decision. It is up to you to consistently and persistently train for your test. Set goals that you personally can attain.

What might stop you from reaching your goal? Identify the obstacles that prevent you from obtaining your goal. Find the necessary resources to overcome those obstacles. Anything worth going after takes investment and commitment. You will be giving up some of your spare time and financial resources, have some aches and pains, be frustrated, and generally wonder why you are studying aikido. It won't come as easy as you may think, but it will come—as long as you don't quit. It is worth overcoming those obstacles. You will have gained valuable skills physically and mentally. You will be proud of yourself, and you just might have found a lifelong place to go and train.

Your Short-Term Objectives

In order to reach your long-term goal, you will need to identify specifically what steps you need to take to achieve it. This requires some honest self-assessment about your beginning point. You will need to assess where you are starting from, where you want to go, and the activities required to get from one to the other.

The short course in establishing a training program consists of two questions and a statement. What do you want? What do you have to do to get it? Do it!

What specific steps do you need to take in each class to reach your goal? In aikido, it is relatively easy to find the short-term objectives. Your school already has set them for you. You will have to learn to trust and follow them. The training program for aikido can appear different from most other training programs. You may need to have your instructor explain to you the structure and curriculum of the class, so you can get the idea that the classes are the step, or short-term objective, to obtaining your long-term goal. To obtain your goal in aikido, show up consistently and train persistently. Be patient.

The secret to reaching a goal is to enjoy the journey getting there.

Your Purpose

Why are you training in aikido? Understand your purpose for training in aikido and what you hope to get out of it, in both the short term and the long term. Know and accept your purpose. Are you training to obtain self-defense skills, exercise, opportunities for social interaction, lessons in discipline and patience, or aikido's philosophical and spiritual benefits? Why are you investing your time and energy in learning aikido? The honest answers to these questions will help you focus on your training goals, objectives, and overall program.

The purpose directs the process of training. The purpose helps set the motivation behind the goals and objectives in training. Your purpose will tell you what you hope to gain by achieving your goal. Know yourself. You are the only person who stops you from achieving success. You are the only one who can make you fail.

Your Process Orientation

Research in sports psychology suggests that once you establish a goal, a good way to achieve it is to forget it. In other words, don't focus on getting that black belt. Focus on the training session you are in. Getting the most out of the process will not only increase the likelihood of achieving your goal, but also give you the opportunity to surpass it. In many sports, you are told not to keep your eyes on the scoreboard, but to keep them on the ball. That's process orientation. Train just to train, and your goal will eventually be achieved. Enjoy the training in every class.

Enjoy the process of training in aikido. Your enjoyment of each class will keep you coming back. It is immediate reinforcement. Eventually the goal and the process become the same. You will train just for the joy of training.

Setting Up a Training Program

Your Learning Stages

Any training program should take into account that there are four stages of learning. This helps you be realistic about your training. The four stages of learning are: unconscious incompetence, conscious incompetence, conscious competence, and unconscious competence.

> The four stages of learning are:
>
> ☞ unconscious incompetence,
>
> ☞ conscious incompetence,
>
> ☞ conscious competence,
>
> ☞ and unconscious competence.

The first stage of unconscious incompetence simply means that what we are doing doesn't work, but we don't know it. Many people, before they start training in aikido, don't know that they don't know what they are doing. You may feel overconfident or may just not worry about not knowing. What you don't know can and will hurt you. The process of change and improvement starts with making the unconscious incompetence conscious.

The second stage is conscious incompetence. This is the stage where you begin to become aware of how much you really don't know. The beginning training in aikido is great for building humility, because you will constantly be shown how much you don't know. For many people, this is a major obstacle to overcome. It is only through an honest admission of what we don't know that we become open to learning.

Many people who have the goal of achieving their black belt discover that this is where the learning and fun really begin. Conscious incompetence is the honest admission that we don't know. The awareness and admission of your incompetence humbles and empties you so that you can begin training to become competent.

The third stage is conscious competence. The techniques you are practicing work, but only when you pay conscious attention to them. This is when you are learning and practicing. This is training. You are learning new skills—pay attention. There is a threshold in learning; if you practice something often enough, it becomes easier until eventually it feels very natural and easy. It is your discipline at this conscious competence stage that makes or breaks your success. Sports psychology and physiology suggest that it may take you from 3,000 to 30,000 realistic repetitions of a specific skill to develop what is called muscle memory of that skill. Be patient with yourself as you train. Don't expect dramatic results to come quickly. With training, the difficult becomes easy. Your mastery of aikido depends on this stage.

Mastery of aikido is a goal and a process of continual learning and practice.

The fourth stage is unconscious competence. After many training sessions, and hours of conscious awareness, the moves seem to happen by themselves. You no longer have to pay conscious attention to what you are doing. At this point, it is locked in. You will simply do it. It takes patience to get to this stage. It is worth it.

In aikido, you can constantly and eternally evolve. Once you have unconscious competence in one part of a skill, you will discover that you have been unconsciously incompetent about another aspect of it. The physical techniques give way to the practice of the principles and philosophy. Aikido is more of a journey than a destination. Enjoy the trip.

Your Mastery

The goal of mastery (Leonard 1992, p. 39), or unconscious competence, takes time and discipline. In the study of mastering physical skills, there is talk of learning curves and plateaus. This translates to the ups, downs, and flat plateaus of learning. First, there is the stage where you are learning a great deal. You are learning constantly, and if you are not too overwhelmed, you will feel excited and will want to learn even more. It is easy to maintain motivation during this stage of the learning curve.

There are times when you will hit a plateau in your learning curve. It just doesn't feel as if you are learning anything new. Training may feel boring and flat. You may consider dropping out. You may feel burnt out. This boring stage is a most important stage.

The plateaus in training are the opportunities to realistically and repetitively, consistently and persistently, practice a technique until it evolves from conscious competence to unconscious competence. This is the time when your discipline wires the technique into your muscle memory. This is the time to get excited about your training. This is when you train your mind as well as your body.

Learning curves have a baseline from which your learning rises and falls. It falls because, when you hit that plateau, you lose interest and train less. You lose some of what you have gained. If you consistently and persistently train during your plateau stage, your new baseline will be the top of your old learning curve. Your height becomes your new baseline, and all new learning starts from there.

Your Realistic Training Schedule

Now that you have set a realistic, long-term training goal with realistic training and short-term training objectives, you need to set a realistic training schedule. How often can you get to your school of choice to train? You have many other commitments in your life besides learning aikido. If your aikido training interferes with other activities you are committed to, you will feel stress for neglecting them and be resentful toward your training. Aikido training should blend with your life in the same way you are learning to blend with your training partner.

Once you have a realistic assessment of the amount of time you can spend on aikido, make a schedule, and commit to it. Once you establish the habit of showing up consistently at your school on certain days, at certain times, you will automatically find yourself there. As you let aikido training blend with your life, it will soon blend with your identity. Aikido becomes not just what you do on a certain day at a certain time, but who you are.

Your Realistic, but High, Training Ethic

As a new student of aikido, you may be surprised to see how many people in class are standing around having social conversations, instead of physically training. This, unfortunately, is very common. There is plenty of time to talk about aikido before and after class. Your time in class is best used by "doing" aikido, not "talking about doing" aikido. Many things are easier to experience first and understand later. The understanding is in the experience, and cannot be gained without it. It is hard to explain in words what the body will learn and know with consistent and persistent training. It is through "doing" aikido that you "become" aikido. A realistic training ethic will allow you to set achievable goals. A high training ethic will help you get the most out of each training experience.

Setting realistic long-term training goals, establishing realistic short-term training objectives, and having a realistic training schedule, with a realistic, but high, training ethic, will help you to be successful in aikido. You need to know what you want to accomplish, what you have to do to get there, and then set about doing it. Once the course is set, and the journey has begun, relax, breathe, and enjoy yourself.

testing for
belt promotion

NITIALLY, aikido did not have a colored belt system that represented rank. The majority of aikido students were already well established in other martial arts and were turning to aikido for both the physical effectiveness and the spiritual philosophy. In many regards, ranking systems were seen as a means of building up the ego identity instead of helping to loosen its grasp on us all. Yet, because of the commercialism of martial arts, there is a need to give frequent reinforcement and reward for achieving a certain level of skill. Aikido began to accept and award colored belts and certificates as marks of rank in the study of aikido. While the rank you receive will be something to strive for and be proud of, please remember that it is only a colored belt. Who you are and your level of competence are more important than your rank.

The Stages of Belt Promotion

In the beginning stages of aikido training, the rank system goes through various levels of *kyu*, or colored belts. Kyu means "class" or "grade" and represents the level of skill and promotion below the black-belt level. Training at the kyu level is learning the basics of aikido, the techniques, and gaining some level of technical skill. Truly, your learning has just begun.

The black belt is only the first of ten levels of *dan*. Training toward your black belt/shodan may seem like an end goal, but it is wiser to see it as another of the stages in your education. Your first-degree black belt (shodan) is like getting your high-school diploma. Your second-degree black belt (*nidan*) is like two years of college, or an associate's degree. Your third-degree black belt (*sandan*) is like four years of college, or a bachelor's degree. Your fourth-degree black belt (*yodan*) is like six years of college, or a master's degree. Your fifth-degree black belt (*godan*) is like eight years of college, or your doctoral degree. Education is ongoing and never ending; so is aikido.

Each stage of your aikido education sets the foundation for the next stage. Aikido training is an ongoing process. Each grade marks your progression along the journey. Some people stop and rest. Some stay at their current level of mastery. Others acquire an enjoyment of the process and a deep appreciation for the accomplishment, and continue.

*B*elt requirements vary. Follow the curriculum set forth by your instructor, school, and affiliation.

Sample Belt Requirements

Each school, instructor, style, federation, and affiliation may require slightly different, but similar, requirements for belt promotions. These examples are only provided to give you some idea of the promotion and rank curriculum. Do not consider them as the absolute requirements. Those are up to your individual system, and may change over time. Requirements, like aikido, evolve with time. The color sequencing of the belts differs also. The usual sequence is white, yellow, orange, green, blue, brown, and black. Your school and affiliation may differ.

Aikikai Hombu Dojo

The Aikikai Hombu Dojo is the home of the World Aikido Federation and the direct descendants and affiliation of O'Sensei Morihei Ueshiba. Here are the testing requirements from the Aikikai Hombu Dojo Grading System (Fujita 1997, pp. 60–61). Each level includes the techniques from all lower levels:

- Fifth kyu (thirty days of training): Shomen-uchi ikkyo, katate-dori shiho-nage, shomen-uchi irimi-nage, suwari-waza kokyu-ho

- Fourth kyu (forty days of training after fifth kyu): Shomen-uchi ikkyo, kata-dori nikyo, yokomen-uchi shiho-nage, shomen-uchi irimi-nage, suwari-waza kokyu-ho

- Third kyu (fifty days of training after fourth kyu): Shomen-uchi ikkyo through yonkyo (seated and/or standing), ryote-dori shiho-nage, yokomen-uchi shiho-nage, shomen-uchi irimi-nage, tsuki irimi-nage, shomen-uchi kote-gaeshi, tsuki kote-gaeshi, ryote-dori tenchi-nage, suwari-waza kokyu-ho

- Second kyu (fifty days of training after second kyu): Shomen-uchi ikkyo through yonkyo (seated and/or standing), katate-dori ikkyo through yonkyo (seated and/or standing), katate-dori shiho-nage (hanmi handachi), shomen-uchi irimi-nage, tsuki irimi-nage, katate-dori irimi-nage, shomen-uchi kote-gaeshi, tsuki kote-gaeshi, katate-dori kote-gaeshi, katate-dori kaiten-nage, ryote-dori tenchi-nage, katate-dori jiyu techniques, suwari-waza kokyu-ho

- First kyu (sixty days of training after second kyu): Shomen-uchi ikkyo through yonkyo, yokomen-uchi ikkyo through yonkyo, katate-dori ikkyo through yonkyo, ushiro ryote-dori ikkyo through yonkyo, yokomen-uchi gokyo, katate-dori shiho-nage (seated and/or standing), ryote-dori shiho-nage (seated and/or standing), shomen-uchi irimi-nage, tsuki irimi-nage, katate-dori irimi-nage, shomen-uchi kote-gaeshi, tsuki kote-gaeshi, katate-dori kote-gaeshi, shomen-uchi kaiten-nage, tsuki kaiten-nage, katate-dori kaiten-nage, ryote-dori tenchi-nage, katate-dori jiyu techniques, ryote-dori jiyu techniques, morote-dori jiyu techniques, kokyu-ho (seated and standing)

- First-degree black belt, shodan (seventy days of training after first kyu; at least fifteen years old): All techniques, seated, hanmi handachi, and standing from men, kata, mune, hiji, te, and ushiro

- Second-degree black belt, nidan (one year after shodan, with 200 days of training): All of the above plus tanto-dori, *futarigake* (two-person attack), and a submission of an article on some aikido-related subject

- Third-degree black belt, sandan (two years after nidan, with 300 days of training): All the above plus *tachi-dori* (sword taking), *jo-dori* (stick or staff taking), *taninzugake* (multiple attack), and an essay regarding aikido (subject will be assigned)

- Fourth-degree black belt, yondan (two years after sandan, with 300 days of practice; at least twenty-two years old): All the above plus jiyu techniques and a short essay.

> Tenshinkai refers to the powerful and flowing style of aikido from Vietnam that O'Sensei personally named "the association of heavenly hearts" or "heaven on earth."

Tenshinkai Aikido

The International Tenshinkai Aikido Federation practices an aikikai style of aikido. Their ranking system is slightly different from the aikikai system, yet contains the same elements. They use the following technique promotion requirements:

- Eighth kyu white belt (three months/thirty-six days of training): Ukemi, aikitaiso, gyaku-hanmi kokyu-nage one and two, shiho-nage, kote-gaeshi, ai-hanmi, kokyu-nage one and two, kote-gaeshi, shiho-nage

- Seventh kyu yellow belt (three months/thirty-six days of training after last promotion): Ai-hanmi ikkyo, nikyo, kokyu-nage three and four, gyaku-hanmi ikkyo, nikyo, kokyu-nage three and four, ryote-dori kokyu-nage one and two, shiho-nage, tenchi-nage, yokomen-uchi shiho-nage, kote-gaeshi, shomen-uchi irimi-nage, ikkyo

- Sixth kyu orange belt (five months/sixty days of training after last promotion): Ai-hanmi sankyo, irimi-nage, kokyu-nage five and six, koshi-nage, gyaku-hanmi irimi-nage, kaiten-nage, kokyu-nage three, four, and five, shomen-uchi nikyo, kokyu-nage one and two, yokomen-uchi kokyu-nage one and two, ikkyo, koshi-nage, ryote-dori ikkyo, kote-gaeshi, kokyu-nage three, four, and five

- Fifth kyu green belt (six months/seventy-two days of training after last promotion): Suwari-waza ikkyo, nikyo, yokomen-uchi ikkyo, nikyo, kokyu-nage, shomen-uchi tenbin-nage, shiho-nage, koshi-nage, kokyu-nage one, two, and three, ryote-dori nikyo, irimi-nage, kokyu four and five, gyaku-hanmi sankyo, kokyu-nage seven, eight, and nine, morote-dori kote-gaeshi, shiho-nage ikkyo, kokyu-nage one, two, and three, mune-tsuki ikkyo, kote-gaeshi, irimi-nage

- Fourth kyu blue belt, one stripe (six months/seventy-two days of training after last promotion): Kata form set two, aiki-jo four techniques, aiki-ken four technique, yokomen-uchi sankyo, kokyu-nage five and six, irimi-nage, morote-dori nikyo, shiho-nage, kokyu-nage one, two, and three, shomen-uchi kokyu-nage four and five, irimi-nage ikkyo, ai-hanmi koshi-nage, kokyu-nage ten and eleven, gyaku-hanmi tenbin-nage, koshi-nage, ryote-dori kokyu-nage six and seven, juji-nage nikyo, tenbin-nage, suwari-waza sankyo, kaiten-nage

- Third kyu blue belt, two stripes (six months/seventy-two days of training after last promotion): Kata forms set three, aiki-jo four techniques, aiki-ken four techniques, ai-hanmi kaiten-nage, kokyu-nage thirteen and fourteen, ushiro-ryote-dori ikkyo, sankyo, kokyu-nage one and two, gyaku-hanmi koshi-nage yonkyo, kokyu-nage ten and eleven, sode-dori shiho-nage ikkyo, nikyo, morote-dori koshi-nage sankyo, kokyu-nage three and four, suwari-waza yonkyo, gokyo, shomen-uchi irimi-nage, kaiten-nage, kokyu-nage four and five, ryote-dori sankyo, yonkyo, koshi-nage, juji-garami, mune-tsuki ikkyo, tenbin-nage, kaiten-nage, yokomen-uchi sankyo, koshi-nage, tenbin-nage, kokyu-nage seven and eight

- Second kyu brown belt, one stripe (six months/seventy-two days of training after last promotion): Aiki-ken four technique, aiki-jo thirty-one-step kata, form, kata form set four, suwari-waza yonkyo, irimi-nage, morote-dori sankyo, tenbin-nage, kokyu-nage five and six, mune-tsuki tanto-tori, nikyo, kote-gaeshi, shomen-uchi kokyu-nage six and seven, tanto-tori, kote-gaeshi, ikkyo, gokyo, yokomen-uchi tanto-tori kote-gaeshi, ikkyo, ushiro-ryote-dori ikkyo, nikyo, shiho-nage, kokyu-nage three and four, ai-hanmi jiyu-waza, gyaku-hanmi juji waza, gokyo, kokyu-nage eleven and twelve, shomen-uchi jiyu waza, yokomen-uchi jiyu waza, mune-tsuki jiyu waza, hanmi-handachi-waza shiho-nage, sankyo, kaiten-nage, kote-gaeshi ikkyo, randori

- First kyu brown belt, two stripes (six months/seventy-two days of training after last promotion; at least thirteen years old): Review all techniques, thirty hours as assistant instructor, kokyu-nage gyaku-hanmi katate-dori, shomen-uchi, morote-dori, ushiro-dori, kokyu-nage ai-hanmi katate-dori, yokomen-uchi, ryote-dori, mune-tsuki, tanto-dori ten waza, mune-tsuki, shomen-uchi, yokomen-uchi, aiki-ken eight-direction, seven waza, aiki-jo thirty-one-step kata, seven waza, kata for four sets, essay of ten pages

Ki-Society

Some of the terminology and labeling of the techniques are different for the Ki-Society than for the aikikai styles of aikido. The Requirements for the Ki-Society are included here for your consideration and education. Shin-Shin Toitsu Aikido Technique Criteria for Promotion (Midland Ki-Society):

- Fifth kyu *shokyu* (thirty hours, three months training): *Udemawashi, ude-furi,* udefuri *choyaku, sayu,* sayu choyaku, ushiro ukemi, ushiro ukemi to standing, *zenpo* kaiten, katate-dori (*kosa-tobikomi*) kokyu-nage, katate-dori tenkan kokyu-nage, kokyu dosa (all ranks), katate-dori ikkyo (irimi and tenkan)

- Fourth kyu (thirty hours after fifth kyu): Ikkyo, *zengo, happo, zenshin-koshin,* kokyu dosa, katatori ikkyo (irimi and tenkan), *munetsuki kote-oroshi,* yokomen-uchi *shiho-nage* (tenkan-irimi, tenkan-tenkan), shomen-uchi kokyu-nage, katate-dori irimi kokyu-nage, katate-tori kokyu-nage (zenpo-nage)

- Third kyu *chukyu* (thirty hours after fourth kyu): *Fune-kogi,* nikyo, sankyo, kote-oroshi, shikko, tenkan, kata-dori nikyo (irimi and tenkan), kata-dori sankyo (irimi and tenkan), kata-dori yonkyo (irimi and tenkan), yokomen-uchi zenpo-nage, ryote-dori zenpo-nage, katate-dori (kosa-tobikomi) kote-oroshi

- Second kyu (fifty hours plus six months after third kyu and instructor's approval): *Kaho* tekubi kosa, *joho* tekubi kosa, ushiro-dori, ushiro-tekubi-dori zenshin, ushiro-tekubi-dori koshin, one *taigi* from numbers 1 through 9, tobikomi ukemi, ushiro-ryote-kubi-dori zenpo-nage, ushiro-katate-dori kubijime sankyo-nage, ryote-dori tenchi-nage (irimi and tenkan), ushiro-dori kokyu-nage (zenpo-nage), ryote-mochi kokyu-nage (*enundo*), katate-dori kaiten-nage (irimi and tenkan), ryote-dori zenpo-nage (three arts), one-person randori

- First kyu (fifty hours plus six months after second kyu and instructor's approval): Hitori waza 1 through 20, two taigi from numbers 1 to 9, suwari-waza handachi shomen-uchi kokyu-nage, suwari-waza handachi mune-tsuki kote-oroshi, suwari-waza handachi yokomen-uchi zenpo-nage, mune-tsuki kokyu-nage zenpo-nage, mune-tsuki kokyu-nage sudori, mune-tsuki kokyu-nage kaiten-nage, katate-dori ryote-mochi kote-oroshi, katate-dori ryote-mochi kokyu-nage (*hachi-no-ji*), yokomen-uchi kote-oroshi (enundo), yokomen-uchi kokyu-nage (hachi-no-ji), shomen-uchi koteoroshi, shomen-uchi ikkyo (irimi and tenkan), ushiro-tekubi-dori koteoroshi, ushiro-tekubi-dori ikkyo, keri waza (three arts), ushiro ryokata-dori, kokyu-nage (three arts), two-person randori, extra techniques, *katameru* (kneeling pin)

- Shodan *jokyu* (seventy hours after first kyu, instructor's approval and chief instructor's approval): Hitori-waza 1 through 20, kokyu ki test, three taigi from 1 to 15 (chosen by examiner), yokomen-uchi (five arts), katate-dori (five arts), ushiro-tekubi-dori (five arts), tanto-dori (five arts), ken gi number one, jo gi number one, four-person randori, ushiro-dori (five arts)

- Nidan (120 hours after shodan, instructor's approval, and chief instructor's approval): Hitori-waza 1 through 20, three taigi from 16 to 23 (chosen by examiner), mune-tsuki (five arts), shomen-uchi (five arts), *tachi-dori* (five arts), ken gi number two, jo gi number two, five-person randori

- Sandan shodan (two years after nidan): All above items, one taigi from 1 to 30 (chosen by examiner), shodan ki test, and all of above showing consistency of mind and body coordination

The Ki-Society also tests ki a number of different ways. They include (1) standing, (2) unbendable arm, (3) thrusting one hand out with weight on the underside, (4) sitting seiza, (5) sitting down and standing up, (6) kokyu-ho, (7) sitting cross-legged while being pushed from behind and with one knee up, (8) thrusting out one hand while being pushed from the wrist, (9) bending backward, (10) stooping, (11) unraisable body, (12) leaning on a partner forward and backward, (13) thrusting out one hand and raising one leg, (14) walking forward while being held, (15) sitting cross-legged while holding both hands from underneath and being pushed by the shoulders, and (16) breathing exercises.

United States Aikido Federation

The United States Aikido Federation also has its own set of basic testing requirements (O'Connor 1993, pp. 82–84). Their system and terminology are similar to the Aikikai Hombu Dojo's system. Again, all the elements are the same:

- Fifth kyu (sixty days of training): Shomen-uchi omote and ura, shomen-uchi irimi-nage, katate-dori shiho-nage omote and ura, ryote-dori tenchi-nage, tsuki kote-gaeshi, ushiro tekubi-dori (both wrists grabbed from behind) kote-gaeshi, morote-dori kokyu-ho

- Fourth kyu (eighty days of training): Shomen-uchi nikyo omote and ura, yokomen-uchi shiho-nage omote and ura, tsuki irimi-nage, ushiro tekubi-dori sankyo omote and ura, ushiro ryokata-dori kote-gaeshi, suwari-waza shomen-uchi ikkyo, suwari-waza kata-dori nikyo omote and ura, suwari-waza kata-dori sankyo omoto and ura.

- Third kyu (100 days after training): Yokomen-uchi irimi-nage (two ways), yokomen-uchi kote-gaeshi, tsuki kaiten-nage, ushiro ryokata-dori sankyo omote and ura, morote-dori irimi-nage (two ways), shomen-uchi sankyo omote and ura, suwari-waza shomen-uchi irimi-nage, suwari-waza shomen-uchi nikyo omote and ura, hanmi handachi (uke standing, nage kneeling) katate-dori shiho-nage and katate-dori kaiten-nage.

- Second kyu (200 days of training): Shomen-uchi shiho-nage, shomen-uchi kaiten-nage, yokomen-uchi gokyo, ushiro tekubi-dori shiho-nage, ushiro tekubi-dori juji-nage, ushiro kubishime (choke from the back while holding one wrist) koshi-nage, morote-dori nikyo, hanmi handachi shomen-uchi irimi-nage, hanmi handachi katate-dori nikyo, hanmi handachi yokomenuchi kote-gaeshi, freestyle (two persons)

- First kyu (300 days of training): Kata-dori men-uchi (five techniques), yokomen-uchi (five techniques), morote-dori (five techniques), shomen-uchi (five techniques), ryote-dori (five techniques), koshi-nage (five techniques), tanto-dori (knife disarming), hanmi handachi ushiro waza (five techniques), freestyle (three persons)

- Shodan (400 days of training): All of first kyu requirements, tachi-dori (bokken, or wooden sword disarms), jo-dori (jo, or stick/staff disarms), henka-waza (combinations), freestyles (four persons)

- Nidan (600 days of training): Attend two seminars a year after shodan, all of shodan requirements, tachi-dori (two persons), freestyle (five persons), kaeshi-waza (counters)

- Sandan (700 days of training): Attend two seminars per year after nidan, subject of examination determined by examiner.

Preparation for, and Participation in, Promotion Testing

There are many things to consider regarding your promotional testing. Your success or failure will depend on how well prepared you are physically and mentally. If you feel prepared in training, the testing situation itself has many performance anxieties that you will need to be prepared for. In the old times, there was only the white belt and the black belt. Everything else was just training. While your testing is important, don't take it too seriously.

Before the testing, there is only the training. After the testing, there is only the training.

Train Physically, Be Prepared

Nothing will help you more in preparing for an upcoming test than to know that you have trained in all the required techniques. There are no shortcuts to physical training. You must put the time in on the mat. Many students mistakenly count up the time they have spent in the school. The quality of your training, and your preparedness for your test, are determined by the actual time you have spent moving and training on the mat. Preparedness does not have to do with how long you have been enrolled or how long it has been since your last promotional test. If you train three times a week, you will probably be better prepared than if you only train once a week. If you spend your time physically training on the mat, you will probably be more prepared than if you spend the same amount of time talking about the techniques. As with all things in life, if you do not show up and actually do the work, don't be surprised if you fail. Likewise, if you do show up and train consistently and persistently, you are ensured of learning the necessary techniques for the promotional test.

The best way to prepare for testing is to train physically and mentally.

The physical promotional testing is exhausting. It requires stamina and cardiovascular conditioning. Running is an excellent cardiovascular activity. Keep a good posture and run as if pulled from your center. Learning to run greater distances is a great way to develop endurance, but also mental toughness. Boxers use a jump rope to build both endurance and lightness on their feet. Run and jump rope slowly at first. Build up a good base of conditioning. Begin to

> If your instructor believes you are ready to test, you probably are. Trust their experience and wisdom.

build variety into your supplemental workouts by doing wind sprints or picking up the pace for short intervals. The steady pace will build up aerobic capacity and endurance. The interval training will build up your anaerobic conditioning and develop power that is more explosive. To train consistently and persistently, and to perform well at a promotional test, you must have stamina and endurance.

Train Mentally

Mental preparation for promotional testing starts the day you start training. At each class, keep in mind why you are there and what you want to get out of it. When you bow before class, use the time to remind yourself. As you bow after class, review what you have learned during that class. Mentally keep your eye on the goal of promotional testing as a step toward achieving your long-term goal. Mentally keep your eye on the class process itself. The goal mentally gives you your direction, the class process gives you the immediate steps or instructions on how to get there.

Relax

Tension is the biggest problem in test taking. You know you are physically and mentally prepared. Tension, in the form of fear and negative thinking, is the best way to choke and fail. Let go of the tension, physically and mentally. Relax the body and calm the mind. Get out of your own way.

Relaxation makes you perform better physically and mentally. The process of relaxation, emphasized throughout this book, is an important characteristic of aikido. If you are relaxed, your body will align better, and your ki will flow better through a relaxed body and a calm mind. Your promotional testing will test more than your physical technique. It will test your acceptance of and competence in the principles of aikido.

Performance

The testing situation itself has many possibilities for performance anxiety. It is important to take into account what you intend to do and the test-taking strategies that can aid your performance and increase your chances of success.

Use the time before your test time to prepare. Get a good night's sleep the night before. Eat a light meal. Show up early. Make sure your uniform is clean. Putting it on will help you get into the right frame of mind.

Respect the formality of the situation. When your time comes to perform, walk slowly and with your back straight. Use the proper posture you have practiced in your training. Show appropriate respect.

Make sure you understand the request or commands given. Under stress, the mind tends to work more slowly and have selective memory. If you don't know, ask to have the request repeated. Do not assume the ready position until you know what you are going to do. The ready position signals your training partner that you want him or her to approach or attack. Wait until you are ready. If you find you are moving incorrectly, finish the technique, acknowledge the error, and begin again.

Make sure you breathe while doing your technique, and move slowly to show that you do know what you are doing. There is a tendency under performance anxiety to speed up. Resist this tendency and go slow. It is better to perform slowly to show the subtleties and deliberateness of the technique than to go too fast and look sloppy.

Between techniques, center yourself. Come back to your center. Take a few deep breaths. Use the resource-anchoring technique from the mental training section. Avoid too much self-criticism and internal dialogue. Let go of the past performance and look forward to the next. Besides helping you to center yourself, handling yourself well between performances demonstrates for the judges that you can apply the aikido principle of flowing. As in randori, let go and move to the next.

You will be judged on how you have handled yourself in training up to this point. You will be judged on how you handle yourself before, during, and after the testing. Make sure that you hold yourself with the dignity that will allow you to look back on your testing performance and be proud of yourself.

Accept Success or Failure Equally

If you do your best, whether you succeed and pass or fail and have to retest, you will have a great learning experience. Sure, it will feel better if you succeed—it's a great boost to your ego and your confidence—but such emphasis on the self is not necessarily the aikido way. Because passing and grading can be an elevator of ego and self-esteem, O'Sensei Morihei Ueshiba did not believe in frequent promotions. Students wore their white belts until promoted to black belts.

Success will teach you what you know. Failure will teach you what you still have to learn. Not passing simply means you get to spend more time training at that level before continuing.

Accept your success or failure as the same. Success and failure are both comments on your progress. Neither is a judgment. Accept both with appreciation for the opportunity, with gratitude for the honest assessment, and with great humility regarding the outcome. They both are a learning experience to further your growth and development.

Train for the Next One

After you have passed your promotional test, enjoy yourself. You have proven that you have consistently and persistently trained and learned the required techniques. The day after your promotion, show up at your school, put on your uniform, and train.

chapter 22
demonstrations

DEMONSTRATIONS are the best way to educate the public about the beauty and power of aikido. There is so much of aikido that is difficult to put into words. Explanations of aikido are often inadequate, but can point the way and be of some small assistance. Aikido is best understood by being experienced. The first of those experiences is visual—you see a demonstration. Very few people know the difference between aikido and other martial arts. Most people believe that all martial arts are the same, with a lot of punching, kicking, and breaking of boards.

Aikido is a great addition to any community event. Aikido's nonviolent approach to conflict prevention, management, and resolution makes it a valuable resource. Look for events in your area and note who is hosting them. Invite others to your school, with your teacher's permission of course, to watch an aikido class in action. Few will fail to issue an invitation in return. You will have the opportunity to share and spread the philosophy, principles, and application of aikido.

Know Your Audience

It is always wise to know who will be witnessing your demonstration. The general public will not be able to see and appreciation the subtleties of more advanced aikido moves. They will not appreciate the sophistication of slowly blending. Some audiences are more interested in the flashy, self-defense applications. Enter and blend with the audience by first giving them something that will appeal to them and get their attention. Gently redirect them to the beauty and power of aikido. More advanced audiences will frown on the flashy techniques, and will see and appreciate the subtleties that demonstrate the principles of aikido, not just the physical techniques.

Show Variety

Show a mixture of attacks and responses, and a mixture of participants. Audiences enjoy seeing the children as well as the adults. They enjoy seeing people whose age, gender, size, and ethnicity they can identify with. Start with one attacker and then build up the number you are using. End with randori. Keep the demonstration short enough so the audience will want more, not so long they get bored. Give them just enough so they are entertained and intrigued.

Enjoy Yourself

Make sure the audience sees that you take aikido seriously, but also that you are having a good time. The joyous nature of practicing and demonstrating aikido allows the audience to have a deeper look at the art.

Plan

Have your demonstrations well choreographed and rehearsed. With the exception of the finale of randori, plan the demonstration well ahead of time. One of the criticisms of aikido is that the demonstrations looked planned. They are. As you have learned through your training, what looks like too much cooperation is only compliance with a well-executed technique and the avoidance of pain and injury. All demonstrations are planned. Make sure you know what you are doing. Nothing interrupts a demonstration more than injuries. It also is not a great way to attract new students. Your demonstration will educate people and advertise aikido.

Have Your Own Announcer

If possible, have your own announcer. It is easier for someone who trains in aikido to explain aikido. The announcer can introduce your group and thank the organizers or host. It is important to give some history, letting people know about O'Sensei Morihei Ueshiba and the training he went through. The announcer can further explain some of the philosophy behind aikido, with its emphasis on budo, harmony, ki, and spiritual values as a way to train and heal a world in chaos and confusion. Many people will not know there are different styles of aikido and will find the aikikai emphasis on technical proficiency and the Ki-Society's focus on ki development interesting. Many in the audience will want to know how to find the right school and what to look for in an instructor. They will want information on the uniform, especially the skirtlike hakama that reminds people of the samurai tradition. Due to the severity of the throws and joint locks, the audience may need to know how to train safely and what to expect of their first days in class. The announcer will be able to illustrate the difference stances, strikes, grabs, throwing techniques, and joint

 At the end of your demonstration, it is polite to bow and say "Domo Arigato Gozaimashita," which means "thank-you" in Japanese.

locks or controlling pins. Many demonstrations begin by showing warmup exercises. As the demonstration progresses, the audience will get an idea of what training is like and how you participate in your workouts. Ki development and mental training are aspects that audiences will not see and appreciate unless they are explained. Most demonstrations have some aspect of self-defense application, to let the audience know that aikido is a powerful and effective martial art, even though it is nonviolent. Most audiences will not understand the belt ranking system or what it takes to progress in aikido. Demonstrations should save randori until the end. Randori makes a great finale to a great demonstration. The announcer can inform the audience that training starts with bowing in respect and ends the same way.

An Attitude of Gratitude

Bow in gratitude for the chance to share your art, invite them to join you, and say good-bye.

Demonstrate your practice to the public so they too can share your joy. Demonstrate the principles and philosophy of aikido by practicing nonviolent conflict resolution and by accepting personal and social responsibility.

glossary

A

Ai: Harmony

Ai-hanmi: Same stance

Aiki: United blending spirit

Aikido: The way of harmony

Aikikai: The original style of aikido that emphasis technical proficiency

Ashi-sabaki: Footwork

Atemi: Strike

B

Bokken: Wooden sword

Budo: Martial ways

D

Daito-ryu: The school or martial art that many aikido techniques are derived from

Dan: Black belt ranking or grade

Do: Way, path

Dogi: Training uniform, often referred to as a gi

Dojo: Training hall

Doshu: Keeper of the way, referring to the son and grandson of O'Sensei

F

Funekogi-undo: Rowing exercise

G

Gokyo: Fifth pinning technique

Gyaku-hanmi: Reverse posture

H

Hakama: Traditional pleated skirt

Hanmi: Oblique stance

Hanmi-handachi: Attacker standing and defender kneeling or seated

Henka: Variation

Hitori-keiko: Solo training

I

Ikkyo: First pinning technique

Irimi: Entering

Irimi-nage: Entering throw

J

Jiyu-waza: Free-style technique

Jo: Stick or staff

Junbi-taiso: Warmup exercises

K

Kaiten-nage: Rotary throw

Kamae: Stance

Katame: Pins or locking

Katate-dori: Held by one hand

Keiko: Training/practice

Ken: Wooden sword

Ki: Energy, spirit

Ki-Society: The style of aikido that emphasizes ki development

Kokyu-ho: Body- and breath-turning exercise

Kokyu-nage: Breath and timing throw

Kote-gaeshi-nage: Wrist turn-out throw

Kyu: Rank or grade prior to black belt (dan)

M

Ma-ai: Distance

Mae-ukemi: Forward roll

Metsuki: Soft eye focus

Morote-dori: Two hands grab one wrist

N

Nage-waza: Throwing technique

Nikyo: Second pinning technique

O

Omote: Front

Omoto: The Shinto cult whose beliefs O'Sensei used as the basis for the spiritual principles of aikido

O'Sensei: Great teacher, affectionately referring to founder Morihei Ueshiba

R

Randori: Multiple person attack training

Rei: Bowing

Ryote-dori: Two-hand grasp

Ryu: School or style

S

Sangen: The triangle, square, and circle that illustrates aikido principles

Sankyo: Third pinning technique

Seiza: Sitting posture

Shayu-undo: Hands-up breath-turning exercise, also refers to a kokyu-nage technique

Shiho-nage: Four-direction throw

Shikko: Knee-walking

Shomen-uchi: Frontal downward strike

Sotaidosa-undo: Partner warmup exercises

Suwari-waza: Seated technique

T

Tachi-waza: Standing technique

Tanto: Knife

Te-gatana: hand blade

Tekubi: Hand shaking, or shaking the spirit

Tenbin-nage: Elbow-lock throw

Tenkan: Circular pivoting footwork

Tori: The person defending; training partner who practices the technique

Tsugi-ashi: Shuffle footwork

Tsuki: Straight forward punch

U

Uke: Training partner who receives the technique

Ukemi: Falling ways, or techniques

Undo: Exercise

Ura: Rear

Ushiro: Behind or from the back

Ushiro-hanten-ukemi: Rolling forward and backward

W

Waza: Technique

Y

Yokomen-uchi: Diagonal strike to head or neck

Yoko-ukemi: Side fall

Yonkyo: Fourth pinning technique

Z

Zanshin: A lingering spirit or connection maintained after physical contact is broken

resources

Books

Dang, Tri Thong. *Beyond the Known: The Ultimate Goal of the Martial Arts*. Boston: Charles E. Tuttle Publishing Company, Inc., 1993.

———. *Towards the Unknown Martial Artist, What Shall You Become?* Boston: Charles E. Tuttle Publishing Company, Inc.,1993.

Dobson, Terry and Miller, Victor. *Aikido in Everyday Life: Giving in to Get Your Way*. Berkeley, Calif: North Atlantic Books, 1993.

Fujita, Masatake. *Aikido Keiki Ho, Aikido Training Method*. The Hague, Netherlands: Stitching Promotie Aikido Nederland, 1997.

Leonard, George. *Master the Keys to Success and Long-term Fulfillment*. New York: Plume/Penguin Group, 1992.

O'Conner, Greg. *The Aikido Student Handbook*. Berkeley, Calif.: Frog Ltd., 1993.

Pranin, Stanley A. *The Aiki News Encyclopedia of Aikido*. Tokyo: Aiki News, 1991.

Tohei, Koichi. *Ki Development Methods: Coordination of Mind and Body*. Tokyo: Ki No Kenkyukai Headquarters, 1973.

Tohei, Koichi. *Book of Ki: Co-ordinating Mind and Body in Daily Life*. Tokyo: Japan Publications, 1976.

Tohei, Koichi. *Ki in Daily Life*. Tokyo: Ki No Kenkyukai Headquarters, 1978.

Ueshiba, Kisshomaru. *The Spirit of Aikido*. New York: Kodansha America, 1984.

Ueshiba, Kisshomaru. *Aikido*. Tokyo: Hozansha Publications, 1985.

Ueshiba, Kisshomaru and Ueshiba, Moriteru. *Best Aikido: The Fundamentals*. New York: Kodansha America, 2002.

Westbrook, A. and Ratti, O. *Aikido and the Dynamic Sphere*. Rutland, Vt.: Charles E. Tuttle Company, Inc., 1970.

Videos

Aikido Journal. *Aiki Expo 2002—Friendship Demonstration Parts One and Two*. Las Vegas, 2002.

Aikikai Hombu Dojo. *Aikido*, Vols. 1–7. Tokyo: World Aikikai Foundation, 1993.

MacYoung, Marc. *Safe in the Streets*. Boulder, Co.: Paladin Press/L.O.T.I. Group, 1993.

Internet

www.AikidoJournal.com (community forum and resources)

www.Aikikai.org (Aikido World Headquarters, Aikikai Foundation, Aikikai Hombu Dojo)

www.AikiWeb.com (community forum and resources)

www.Iwama-Aikido.com (Iwama Aikido)

www.Ki-Aikido.net (Ki-Society)

www.Seidokan.org (Seidokan Aikido)

www.Tomiki.org (Tomiki Aikido)

www.USAikiFed.com (United States Aikido Federation)

www.YoseikanAikido.com (Yoseikan Aikido)

www.Yoshinkan-Aikido.org (Yoshinkan Aikido)

THE TUTTLE BASICS SERIES

The books in the Tuttle Basics series provide a complete introduction to the martial arts and health and fitness techniques. All of the books in the series are meant to coach beginning students through their first six months of practice—and beyond. These books allow students to gain a complete understanding of these arts from the very beginning, helping them progress faster and with a clearer vision of purpose.

TAEKWONDO BASICS
by Scott Shaw
50 b&w photographs • 6³/₄ x 9³/₄ 192 pp
$12.95 paperback • ISBN: 0-8048-3484-9

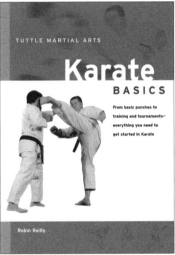

KARATE BASICS
by Robin Rielly
50 b&w photographs • 6³/₄ x 9³/₄ 192 pp
$12.95 paperback • ISBN: 0-8048-3493-8

Jeet Kune Do Basics
by David Cheng
50 b&w photographs
6³/₄ x 9³/₄ 192 pp
$12.95 paperback • ISBN: 0-8048-3542-X

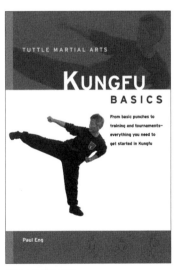

Kungfu Basics
by Paul Eng
50 b&w photographs
6³/₄ x 9³/₄ 192 pp
$12.95 paperback • ISBN: 0-8048-3594-6

OTHER MARTIAL ARTS TITLES TO ENJOY

by A. Westbrook and O. Ratti

AIKIDO AND THE DYNAMIC SPHERE
An Illustrated Introduction
by Adele Westbrook and Oscar Ratti
over 300 b&w drawings
6 x 9 384 pp
$24.95 paperback • ISBN: 0-8048-3284-6
$32.95 hardcover • ISBN: 0-8048-0004-9

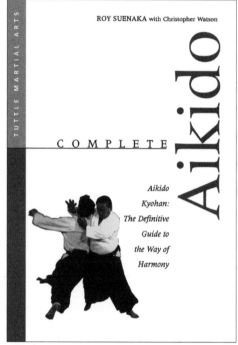

COMPLETE AIKIDO
The Definitive Guide to the Way of Harmony
by Roy Suenaka and Christopher Watson
400 b&w photos
6 x 9 416 pp
$19.95 paperback • ISBN: 0-8048-3140-8

For a **complete listing** of all **MARTIAL ARTS books**,
visit our website at www.tuttlepublishing.com